Talking Back and Looking Forward

Talking Back and Looking Forward

An Educational Revolution in Poetry and Prose

Edited by
Paul C. Gorski
Rosanna M. Salcedo
Julie Landsman

ROWMAN & LITTLEFIELD
Lanham • Boulder • New York • London

Published by Rowman & Littlefield
A wholly owned subsidiary of The Rowman & Littlefield Publishing Group, Inc.
4501 Forbes Boulevard, Suite 200, Lanham, Maryland 20706
www.rowman.com

Unit A, Whitacre Mews, 26-34 Stannary Street, London SE11 4AB

British Library Cataloguing in Publication Information Available

Library of Congress Cataloging-in-Publication Data

Names: Gorski, Paul, editor of compilation. | Salcedo, Rosanna M., 1972–, editor of compilation. | Landsman, Julie, editor of compilation.
Title: Talking back and looking forward : an educational revolution in poetry and prose / edited by Paul C. Gorski, Rosanna M. Salcedo, Julie Landsman.
Description: Lanham : Rowman & Littlefield, [2016]
Identifiers: LCCN 2015040869 (print) | LCCN 2015047761 (ebook) | ISBN 9781475824896 (hardcover : alk. paper) | ISBN 9781475824902 (pbk. : alk. paper) | ISBN 9781475824919 (electronic)
Subjects: LCSH: Educational equalization—United States. | Multicultural education—United States. | Social justice—United States. | Educational equalization—Poetry. | Multicultural education—Poetry. | Social justice—Poetry.
Classification: LCC LC213.2 .T35 2016 (print) | LCC LC213.2 (ebook) | DDC 379.2/6—dc23
LC record available at http://lccn.loc.gov/2015040869

∞ ™ The paper used in this publication meets the minimum requirements of American National Standard for Information Sciences Permanence of Paper for Printed Library Materials, ANSI/NISO Z39.48-1992.

Printed in the United States of America

For Mom and Dad, who nurtured in me the love of poetry and music and the inability to distinguish one from the other.
—Paul

For my children, Javier and Manuel, my greatest teachers.
—Rosanna

With gratitude to my son and husband, both social justice advocates, who keep me grounded.
—Julie

Contents

Foreword: Voices for Diversity and Social Justice

Antonia Darder

Often when the radical voice speaks about domination we are speaking to those who dominate. Their presence changes the nature and direction of our words. —bell hooks (1989)

I begin here with bell hooks's words about the radical voice, in that the editors of this volume have courageously taken on an enormous task, with precisely that desire to create a place where previously unheard or silenced voices of teachers might find an opportunity to speak freely and unencumbered. What has made this possible, given hooks's powerful warning, is that the editors have opened the academic field of expression, so that contributors to this volume might speak through a medium of expression—whether prose, poetry, photography, or art—that encompasses their truth about their quest to respond to the unjust conditions at work in the lives of their students. An uncompromising call for political transformation weaves the collection together with coherence and brilliance. What becomes fully apparent, as one moves through the volume, is the multidimensional ways in which teachers not only understand the larger educational struggle in which they are immersed, given the oppressive conditions that persist within schools, but also the incredible sensibilities they bring to their teaching and their relationships with students.

As an educator for social justice who has persisted in the field for more than three decades, reading this collection is a formidable reminder that teachers are indeed doing amazing things each day, contrary to the popular belief that they are failing our children. Instead, what becomes instantly clear, from the very beginning, is that teachers, too, are oppressed by the tyranny of standards and an instrumentalized and meritocratic system of education that interferes with their social agency, often negating their legitimate concerns regarding school life and the destructive impact of particular accountability practices upon their students—particularly students from economically impoverished and racialized communities. For these teachers, education is not only a human right but also a politically transformative process that must support the humanity and empowerment of teachers, students, parents, and communities alike.

It is refreshing to read a volume where the voices of those seldom heard or seldom consulted about the conditions of their own labor find a place to express the anguish, grief, struggles, and triumphs of their labor within schools. Their reflections on social justice speak to so many issues that now have been mostly eliminated from discussion in the neoliberal climate of accountability. Nevertheless, these teachers persist in their pedagogical efforts and their commitment to stand up and speak against the many injustices that debilitate the intellectual formation of our children, both within schools and out in the world. Moreover, an understanding that our conversations about education must stretch in ways that move us beyond the politics of containment and toward greater open and honest dialogue is at the heart of what this volume provides during this difficult moment in our history.

CRITICAL INSIGHTS FROM TEACHERS WHO DARE TO LOVE

We must dare, in the full sense of the word, to speak of love without fear of being called ridiculous, mawkish, or unscientific, if not antiscientific. . . . We must dare so that we can continue to teach for a long time under conditions that we know well: low salaries, lack of respect, and the ever-present risk of becoming prey to cynicism. We must dare to learn how to dare in order to say no to the bureaucratization of the mind to which we are exposed every day.—
Paulo Freire (1989)

The stories, poems, and art in this book reflect in a myriad of ways Freire's insistence that we dare to love as we carry out our labor as teachers within the classroom and communities. The critical insights expressed here in bits of poems, images, essays, and stories recounted can assist teachers committed to social justice to understand that they are not alone in this great struggle for educational transformation. Instead, through the voices of contributors, teachers will find both solace and nourishment, which can support their own efforts to unveil, challenge, and transform unjust policies and practices that seek to rob our children and communities of both dignity and the belief in our human capacity for self-determination. With this in mind, I want to point to some of the most striking ideas found in this volume.

Interrupting Commonsensical Prescriptions

The collection opens with Beaton's short story "Regrouping the Children," which strikes at the heart of commonsensical ideas that imprison our thinking and prevent us from transforming the ways we understand students and their responses in the classroom. In concert, Galt's poem "Quick Spring" exemplifies the tendencies of teachers to essentialize in deficit ways the abilities and capacities of students from oppressed communities, leaving these teachers in sheer disbelief when a student's work blatantly defies their prescriptive expectations.

The Power of Everyday Life

Many of the pieces included in the collection point to what is not taught in schools; that is, the knowledge and political power of being truly embodied in our everyday realities or, as Sayler concludes, the "victory of cooking pots and combs." Through integrating the lived experiences of students and their communities within the classroom, teachers can address *what really matters* or, as Nash notes, the "truth that's already there." This is to say that often-negated cultural wisdom at work in their everyday lives of both students and teachers can serve them well to build together empowering ways of thinking and engaging the social inequalities and exclusions they face in the world. Hence, we find great power in the testimonials of these teachers, particularly to the extent that they move students' everyday lives to the center of classroom teaching and learning, whether it be in the context of history, art, science, or math, as Durairajan's piece well illustrates.

Humility and Commitment When Not Knowing

Beginning from the place of *not knowing*, as Gorski describes in his essay, genuinely speaks to the humility and commitment required of us to enter into a cultural worldview that is not our own and, thus, unknown but that still beckons us to enter, so that we may better connect and understand the beauty and humanity of students whose cultural and class worldviews may be very distinct from our own. Rather than seeing our students as deficient beings, teachers in this volume acknowledge repeatedly the rich knowledge that students bring and our responsibility as educators committed to social justice to expand and explore *with* them territories of difference that can lead us all to new ways of thinking and knowing one another, as well as the world we share.

The Tyranny of Standards

Stone's poem "Standardized" and the notion of "testing overload" expressed succinctly in Roberts's haiku speak to the dreadful educational conditions that strip children, from a very early age, of their innocence and freedom to learn. Several of the contributors call out the tyranny of standardization, as instances and mechanisms of educational oppression are powerfully unveiled in their works. Through heart-wrenching evidence grounded in the everyday struggles of students and teachers alike, authors point to meritocratic practices that both dispirit and weaken the epistemological curiosity of students to know their world. In a variety of ways, the futility of reforming a broken educational system is foregrounded here, in the midst of tales of great courage and perseverance by teachers who genuinely seek to embody a pedagogy of love while challenging, as does Olivas, a politics of reform "full of profit yet no promise" or, for Jocson, the disfigurement of school rules.

Belief in the Possibility of Transformation

So many poignant bits of lives shaped by anguish are brought to light here but with a radical sense of hope and faith that teachers, students, and communities working together can indeed transform conditions of social inequalities and exclusions—and, as Stein writes, become truly "phoenixes reborn" in the quest for a more just world. In McCullers's poem, there is a sense that rebirth must be linked to our capacity to connect organically with nature and only through so doing can we discover the "right thing to do" with our students or enact practices that truly respect the dignity of their existence as subjects of their own lives. In seeking to construct emancipatory pedagogical moments with her students, Zawinski engages the power of memory in her poem, while Audley-Piotrowski, as do other authors, points to the difficult political formation that teachers must be willing to undergo if they are to better understand the truth about their students' lives and its significance to an emancipatory approach to teaching—one that humanizes and transforms classroom inequalities rather than perpetuates them.

A Decolonizing Sensibility of Resistance

Jimenez's satirical apology is also a deeply tender and heartbreaking exposé of his own experience with racism and colonialism's banking education (Freire 1970). Historical forms of oppression of indigenous people must be understood within a long historical trajectory that encompasses the consequences of slavery and colonization in the lives of racialized working-class students (Darder 2012). Here, as in other places, the impact of ancestral memory and the tenacity of native culture and language that "refuse to die" speaks to a decolonizing sensibility of resistance that must be embraced by teachers and students as we work together to problematize the destructive conditions that shape the lives of oppressed peoples in this country and around the world. This, of course, is also signaled in Gabriel's "A Classroom Assignment," where a debate on "illegal immigrants" uncovers the shrouded stereotypes of Mexicans embedded deeply in commonsensical notions internalized, as well as the manner in which categories are used to divide human beings, often limiting our understanding of the profound human interdependence that must inform our emancipatory struggles.

Voices That Speak to the Pain

Another powerful dimension in this collection are the voices that speak to the unacknowledged and embodied pain and anguish that persists in the lives of teachers and students from culturally and economically oppressed communities. Alhady's words, "when I scream out of pain / you look at me surprised" and Sapigao's poem "Felipe," as well as La-Marche's "unpredicted storm," all express facets of suffering that often go unheard and unseen. This discussion also raises concerns about how communities of color are monitored, surveilled, and "othered" in an *abyssal divide* (Santos 2014), where our failure or unwillingness to acquiesce or assimilate to the dominant culture renders us (and our pain) completely invisible and nonexistent. Testimonies of teaching here also reflect the struggle to believe that *another education is possible*, one that permits us to read the maps of ourselves, as expressed in Warren's "Pickled," without censorship or repercussions. In distinct but also similar ways, the authors speak about the contradictions and conflicts that must be engaged as teachers seek to move beyond the neat and tidy definitions of the status quo, which falsely bombard students daily with an instrumentalizing curriculum and media that function to fabricate their limited desires.

Unveiling Gender Politics

Harlan-Ferlo's contribution, "Look," uses the rules of clothing as a powerful metaphor to speak to the oppression of sexism and patriarchal rule, which demands that women's knowledge and power remain forever covered and inaccessible, even to ourselves. Further, Cherry-McDaniel's "Teaching from the Margins" engages how violence against women has become so normalized or justified that students fail to note its presence when manifested in the curriculum. Her efforts to engage this phenomenon—as it unfolds in the classroom—illustrates the difficulty, conflicts, and contradictions that make teaching *against the grain* an arduous yet necessary strategic endeavor. Moreover, we are drawn to recognize that the power of participation and self-vigilance must be at the heart of teacher efforts to build classroom community with students in order to open the field for critical inquiry and critique—essential to our personal and communal transformation. Racism and gender resurface in Sulé's "Three Spaces of Exclusion," which powerfully illustrates the multiplicity and interrelatedness of oppression in the lives of women of color who do not fit the Barbie-doll prototype of the dominant culture. Gilbertson's "They Said," too, raises issues of the body and the responses it generates when it does not comply, as well as the struggle to resist these responses. In each of these examples, racism, sexism, and body politics comingle in ways that remind us that we cannot effectively contend with one form of oppression without engaging the many others that constantly intersect.

Personal Formation and Openness to Serious Truth

Enloe's "Oasis of Peace" reminds us that the labor for emancipatory education and our capacity to embrace difference actually begins, foremost, within ourselves as we extend ourselves as subjects out into the world of our classrooms and communities. Similarly, teacher willingness to speak and to hear "some serious truth" is how Busman terms the willingness to engage openly with our students' stories of "border crossing," which transgress or push the boundaries of prevailing social norms of acceptable or appropriate classroom conversation, given the limited terrain of mainstream views of legitimate creative writing and social action. And as teachers open up to difficult and painful stories of students' lived experiences, we are reminded that we must be courageous — particularly when the tremendous power of their stories of oppression flood us, causing perplexity, sorrow, uncertainty, and bewilderment.

Language and Creativity as Weapons for Struggle

In reading this wonderful collection, it is remarkable how all the authors, each in their unique way, illustrate Montreal's notion that "language is a weapon" for social justice. Our labor for justice requires teachers to be willing to access, then, whatever skills and resources are available to us so that we may *speak truth to power* while we simultaneously create a place for the silenced histories of those never consulted to move to the center of the discourse. Our very survival as liberatory educators demands that we bring this commitment to our construction of knowledge and the exercise of our praxis in the name of democratic life. In doing so, we must also recognize that this is complicated, particularly when we contend with Audre Lorde's (1997) caution that we cannot liberate ourselves "using the master's tool." Hence, in writing our own stories and speaking our own truths, the traditional discursive tools of the master's language must be transformed in our own image, through our creativity as empowered historical subjects. This is key to teaching against the grain in that there is no way that we can teach that which we ourselves do not understand or do not enact in our own lives.

Fighting for Justice by Learning the Lessons

The difficulty and expansiveness of our task can never be lost on us, as it is not lost on Myhre in "Starfish," where he comes to recognize that his task is "not to make a difference" but rather "to fight, with everything I have." However, to accomplish this, we must believe in the value of our lives and our labor as teachers in a world and as people who were truly not meant to survive (Lorde 1997). Thus, we must learn to live with the "battle scars decades long," as Gonzales notes in "All the Ways We Learn." Teachers' bodies and hearts are so often marked by territories of anguish and disappointment yet also by the powerful lessons that are learned along the way, despite our suffering. I would say that learning to find the lesson in the most wretched moments of struggle has been the saving grace that has allowed me to survive thirty-five years in this work for educational justice. And, most importantly, this seems to have been the saving grace for the teachers here, whose writings and stories bear witness to the strength and beauty of teachers committed to constructing emancipatory possibilities *with* their students.

When Enough Is Enough

For Thomas, finally declaring "enough was enough" with oppressive educational practices opened the door to a classroom where "soon the pleasures became many / as varied as the children themselves." Throughout the stories, poems, images, and truths spoken in this volume, there is a recognition that we must access our social agency *in combination* with what hooks (1994) calls the "authority of experience" if we are to build critical social consciousness in the name of genuine inclusion and difference. That is, where the historically oppressed are no longer expected to become social imitations of the oppressor, assuaging their fears and comforting their anxieties. Rather, our classroom labor should support students of color to become self-determining subjects of their own destinies, where, as Hayes asserts, they can tell us "Use my words." This speaks to a process that moves beyond domestication and indoctrination, as Schnoeker-Shorb affirms, to a place where teachers can truly reach across the abyssal divide to intimately connect with students' hopes and dreams. In the process, however, we must face, as did Levine, the angst of "The Goddess of Autumn" as she pleas for her children, who must endure the consequences of the debilitating conditions of oppression that shape their lives.

Reframing Pain through Social Connection

In concrete ways, authors speak to how we must connect more intimately to our students through, as Bintliff asserts, "reframing pain into resiliency and activism." Learning and struggling with our students in the classroom requires that we sincerely permit them to touch our lives and be willing to be touched and changed by their interventions into ours. It is through such an intimate relational pedagogy of love that we become more able to grapple deeply with our own shortcomings and, thus, support and guide our students through their intellectual and social processes, as well. It is also in this way that we recognize that our communal learning within the classroom constitutes rich fodder for our social struggle out in the world—in that our classrooms are, in fact, social and political expressions of the real world.

Significance of Love

One of the greatest contributions to education that Paulo Freire made was his consistent effort to articulate a pedagogy of love (Darder 2015). The significance of love in the critical pedagogical process of teachers committed to justice is at the heart, for example, of Landsman's poem, "Praise," where the spirit of tenderness extends courageously not in the easy moments of students' lives but in those moments when life in the classroom and beyond make loving nearly impossible—but absolutely necessary to transform the conditions of oppression that deny our humanity. Echoes of this phenomenon also reverberate profoundly in Beaton's "Three Portraits," Turman's essay "Willie Alexander," and Jenkins's poem "Breaking Free."

Challenging Pretense and Embracing Honesty

The collection continues with "School Talk," an essay that moves us through four short stories about students in a school written from the vantage point of a retired school secretary. Most striking about this piece is the manner in which secretaries and other school staff are generally left completely out of important discussions about students' lives and yet how much they often see and understand about the conflicts and contradictions at work, particularly when it comes to the ways in which school language is used as a pretense for change. In this sense, language exists as a sort of deceptive vehicle within educational institutions that must be deconstructed and challenged in our teaching. Similarly, Warren's "letter to student" challenges the "lies . . . in the absence," reminding us that teaching for social change requires the undoing of lies and learning to relieve "this clump in my throat [that] is your honesty."

TOWARD A COLLECTIVE VOICE FOR JUSTICE

"A Litany of Survival" by Audre Lorde (1997, 255–56)

And when the sun rises we are afraid
it might not remain
and when the sun sets we are afraid
it might not rise in the morning
when our stomachs are full we are afraid of indigestion
when our stomachs are empty we are afraid
we may never eat again
when we are loved we are afraid
love will vanish
when we are alone we are afraid
love will never return
and when we speak we are afraid
our words will not be heard
nor welcomed
but when we are silent
we are still afraid
So it is better to speak,
remembering
we were never meant to survive.

True to the spirit of this book, there is something astoundingly powerful when we join our stories of struggle to create a genuinely collective voice for justice. In concert with this political commitment of solidarity, I offer a small bit of my story and a poem to the mighty voices of struggle that unfold in this volume and, thus, represent outstanding contributions to the literature on diversity and social justice in education.

My Political Formation

My process of political formation and radicalization has truly challenged me in fierce and unpredictable ways to contend with the hidden structures that perpetuate policies and practices of inequality in our lives and our communities, through our classroom teaching and community work. By so doing, this has allowed my labor with students to deepen our pedagogical visions of social justice within schools and the larger society in which we reside. However, it cannot be denied that this has been a long and arduous journey. Yet, what has allowed me to survive and thrive has always been a deep sense of justice that has prevailed in my life and continues to inspire both my teaching and my everyday relationships. Moreover, it has been through very difficult moments in my lived history that a deep spiritual process has connected my being and my knowing with the suffering and struggle of others, as I have attempted in community to make sense of a world that was not constructed for our survival in that it was not meant for the survival of oppressed populations.

As a working-class woman of color, my many years in the field of education have been at times a real nightmare—in that I have often been forced to contend with deeply embedded notions and practices of deficit that have demanded of me, and others like me, far more than our privileged colleagues yet have measured us with the same yardstick. Seldom was there the recognition that the achievements of working-class women of color, for example, required from us two or three or four times the amount of work to receive the same respect and recognition. In the process, I came to realize that teaching for social justice was not a vocation for the faint of heart. Instead, it has required commitment, courage, and coherence, despite moments of utter exhaustion, in order to push against those barriers of civilized oppression, entrenched in an institutional culture of denial—that wittingly or unwittingly has functioned to stubbornly conserve structures and relationships of inequality, particularly within the arena of education and creative work. As such, very good people have been so ensconced in their commonsensical privilege that they could not help but respond in ways that either have demanded my sameness or pushed for my rejection.

Hence, paradoxically, it has been through persistently challenging those ideologies and social and material conditions of inequality that I have found with others the strength to persevere. By embracing a loving spirit of transgression, in defiance of those artificial boundaries erected by racism, patriarchy, and class privilege, many of us found our voice, energy, coherence, and integrity with which to launch a body of *scholarship by the oppressed* that could speak to our lives without negating the brutal impact that legacies of slavery, colonization, and genocide—seen today in the guise of poverty, miseducation, and incarceration—have had and continue to have on communities of color in this country and around the world.

Often my perspective has been violently silenced and fiercely marginalized, as it has been for many of the authors in this volume. However, the ideas voiced in this book well illustrate that it is precisely because of the power of our teaching, scholarship, and activism as social justice educators that we are all able to speak these words here, with both love and hope that, in the very near future, all educational institutions and societies will genuinely embrace the multidimensionality of our humanity, so that our everyday survival will no longer be tenuous or uncertain and our children can truly become equal and respected stewards of the world.

The Transformative Power of the Poetic

Whether through my teaching, my art, or my poetry, these have been the values and politics that have deeply informed my continuing educational labor and community activism for human rights, social justice, and economic democracy. In so many ways, I also perceived such values resounding loudly in the authors' voices and their expressed transformative commitment. So in the spirit of this radical political endeavor, I conclude with a poem and my profound faith in the transformative power of the poetic.

Rican woman madness is just another word for love.

Rican-woman-madness
is just another word for love,
she is born of the chains of slavery
and the genocidal history of the Taíno
brushing furiously against
the backdrop of Spanish barbarism.

She is a fighter, warrior blood
oozes through her veins, fills
her womb and exits willfully
through the pounding of her heart.

She will have no qualms about
throwing out the man she loves,
if he comes swinging at her
with the metaphoric machete
of a hateful tongue.

No man who has loved a Rican woman
can forget the wicked lustfulness
and blessed grace of her sensuality,
she makes love in the living.

In her sacred land of histérica
(as we are often proclaimed),
no human emotion is denied,
all are welcomed and pursued
for the sheer pleasure of their sensation
rip roaring from our toes to the
ends of our frizzified Rican hair.

Rican woman's rage runs deep,
but her love runs deeper,
she is the sensibilities of the
moon, sky, and earth combined,
they penetrate into the very core
of all lives natural existence
transmitting and receiving
a million and one universal vibrations
coming and going all at the same time.

The Rican woman is a wild woman,
it is true that she has been colonized
by the rabid thieves who stole her land,
and twisted her history to unrecognizable
proportions, but still and yet,
she refuses to be colonized in the spirit
and will fight to the death to protect
the integrity of the people's song.

But be not the fool and make no mistakes,
the Rican woman is about life and death,
if you desire death she will surely comply
with the fury of the betrayed on a killing rampage,
if you desire life, she will clearly oblige
with her sweet and wild Rican-woman-madness way.

The Rican woman
does not hold her tongue,
she will not permit you to toy
with the passion of her existence,
she refuses submission,
she will speak loudly until
she is buried underground,
and then she will return
to haunt you in your dreams.

The magical whiff of her presence

refuses to leave the scene once she is gone,
it will stay upon your clothes,
it will saturate your hair,
it will permeate your very being,
she will never let you forget that she exists.

So don't be deceived
by the Rican assimilated versions
who curtsey and roll around in the
bureaucratic red tape in disguise,
underneath the white-washed facade
hides a wild island spirit
that will not be domesticated,
weeping ceaselessly to be released.
Rican woman embraces her power as
the motherhood of all creations,
and she will follow the sweet sounds
of her children or her lover calling
"aye mamita" to the ends of the world.

In her negrita self, she is a vessel of love
and shimmering, unadulterated truth,
her truth is of radiant ebony black,
she is not of the sterilized, sophisticated
purity of the etherealized white light,
she is about gutsy, grimy, earthy truth,
the kind that is found beneath the thickness
of old toenails, in the very pit of underarms,
within the folds of fleshy skin, and between
the musty scent of warm full thighs,
hers is a truth of no return, no compromise,
that liberates and frees enslaved black and
brown brothers and sisters who weep
and pray and sing to Changó in the dark.

Rican-woman-madness is just another form of love
that is so easily misunderstood, feared, and
tyrannized by those who do not know how to
read the vital signs of a Rican-woman-madness,
a love that lives in the midst of anguish and joy,
all wrapped up together in the urgency and
delight of her salsa island gyrations.

Rican woman is a volcano,
her anger is legitimate

for she is tired of the bullshit
cover-up reality of a so-called
culturally diverse rhetorical world,
her struggle is legitimate
for she cannot live in a world of pretense
and colorized marginalization,
her love is legitimate,
for she cannot live in a world of lies.

Rican-woman-madness
is just another word for love,
a love that needs open, flowing life in
all its shapes and far reaching dimensions,
a love that will accept nothing but today
and refuses to be appeased with
translucent promises of tomorrow,
a love that will no longer tolerate the forces
of human cruelty and injustice,
a redemptive love that is completely
stripped naked and fully present
just for the asking,
(if you dare).

REFERENCES

Darder, A. 2012. *Culture and Power in the Classroom.* Boulder, CO: Paradigm.
———. 2015. *Freire & Education.* New York: Routledge.
Freire, P. 1970. *Pedagogy of the Oppressed.* New York: Seabury.
———. 1989. *Teachers as Cultural Workers.* Boulder, CO: Westview.
hooks, b. 1989. *Yearnings: Race, Gender, and Cultural Politics.* Minneapolis: Consortium Books.
———. 1994. *Teaching to Transgress.* New York: Routledge.
Lorde, A. 1997. *The Collected Poems of Audre Lorde.* New York: Norton.
Santos, B. de Sousa. 2014. *Epistemologies from South.* Boulder, CO: Paradigm.

Introduction

For us, choosing a career in education meant something more than merely selecting a profession. It was a calling of sorts: a call to service, a call to justice. As artists we have experienced a similar call to put our creative passions to work in the name of justice.

In our view, education, like art, is transformational. We believe that access to the transformative potentials of education—good, critical, deeply engaging education—is a fundamental human right. In this way, all educators are agents for social justice. Sure, we all could be doing other things. We could find jobs with greater material rewards and more prestige and less scrutiny. We choose education because it's important—we *know* it's important.

We also know that the ideal of education as a public good is in serious peril. In the United States, and increasingly elsewhere, profiteers less interested in the human right of education than in finding ways to make public spheres into financial opportunities are wresting more and more control of teaching out of the hands of teachers, often with the help of the politicians whose campaigns they fund. High-stakes testing. Hyperaccountability. Corporate-run charter schools. As agents for social justice, we always have felt a sense of responsibility to respond to these conditions.

We respond, in part, through teaching. Despite the imposition of bad educational policy, teachers around the country are doing amazing things. They are cultivating critical and creative thinking, challenging the corporate takeover of public education, refusing to test their students to sleep. Despite these efforts, the educational system is designed increasingly to favor that which it deems "standard," as defined by policy makers who may or may not have any training in human development or educational theory and who, more to the point, may have no idea what it's like to teach. Do these decision makers consider the wide range of students we serve? Do they have any idea at all how the most marginalized youth experience school?

We assembled this book in order to highlight the voices of those who do have an idea—of people who have experienced or witnessed the impact of educational injustice on the lives of marginalized youth and the educators who advocate for them. We set out to collect writing about people's experiences—their reflections on social justice and injustice, equity and inequity in and out of schools that influence educational access and opportunity. By sharing our stories in poetry and prose and photography, telling our truths either as people on the margins or as their partners in struggles for educational justice, it is our intention to expand the narrative of educational policy and practice. We hoped to create space for the voices of people who are rarely consulted about what works and what needs to improve in schools; about how neoliberal school reforms are taking the heart out of public education; about the atrocities of high-stakes testing, hyperaccountability, and inflexible standardization; about the disempowerment and deprofessionalization of teachers; about the criminalization of youth and the lack of adequate resources in many of the schools and school systems in the United States.

We asked contributors to stand up and to speak out. We asked them to talk back to the conditions that are deteriorating public schools, that are making it more and more difficult to teach in the ways we know are most effective for youth. We asked them to challenge troubling school reform initiatives head on, to expose explicit and implicit forms of racism and heterosexism and economic injustice and other oppressions, to name the best and the worst of what they're seeing in schools.

"Don't mince words," we pleaded.

They didn't mince words, we think you'll agree.

The stories contained in this book stretch the conversation on educational policy and practice by revealing, using the tools of creative expression, what school looks and feels like to the most marginalized youth and their teachers.

We hope it will encourage you, too, to stand up, talk back, speak out, and be heard.

Part One

Troubling Common Sense

Photographer Katrina Ohstrom has focused for the past several years on visually documenting the impact of austerity measures and free-market education reform. Using the backdrop of long-vacant public school buildings, newly shuttered classrooms, and school nurses' offices, Ohstrom challenges her audience to draw their own conclusions about the state of childhood, equality, and education in the United States today. The photographs at the beginning of each part were taken in association with this project. More of Katrina's photography can be found at OhstromPhoto.com.

ONE

Regrouping the Children

by Anne Beaton

(Inspired by Raymond Carver's "Popular Mechanics")

Earlier that day, the temperature hovered above freezing. Thick clouds smeared together into a solid gray backdrop that absorbed all color and light. Outside, the world took on the look of a monochromatic photograph. But it was becoming black and white on the inside, too.

He was hastily jotting on a school-issued memo pad as she entered the room. "We have an idea," he said and slid the sheet across the table.

A tight grid announcing four teacher names along the top and framed by *M, T, W, Th, F* down the left-hand side of the paper held captive four groups of regrouped children: *1, 2, 3, 4* displayed in a comforting but confining pattern that rotated within its boxes.

"It's not working," he said. "Any change is better than continuing with what's not working."

"What's not working?" she said.

"The kids," he said. "The kids aren't working."

"So, you would like to create groups," she said. She pressed her pointer-finger and thumb down on the paper and spun it toward herself.

"Yes," he said, "regrouped groups."

"How would you like to regroup the children?" she said. She rose up from her seat and moved toward the whiteboard, grabbing a black dry-erase marker.

"Quiets and Won'ts," he said. He crossed his arms against his chest and tilted back slightly in the office chair.

"Quiets and Won'ts," she said. "So, behaviors," she said, writing the word *behavior* on the board and underlining the word with a faded black mark. "But you have four groups," she said. "Can you think of any other behaviors that children exhibit in the classroom?"

"Disruptive," he said. "Compliant."

His arms, still crossed, rose and fell with each breath. She added the words beneath the other two. The worn black strokes balanced along a continuum of gray as she wrote.

"And," she said.

He unfolded his arms and picked up his pencil from the table. He rolled the pencil between his fingers and took one glance at the clock. She waited.

"Well," he said, "the three Cs." He leaned forward in his chair, causing the wheels to protest quietly under his weight.

She stood with the marker in her hand. Her eyes fixed on the smudged whiteboard where earlier that day she had recorded data for teachers who questioned the validity of their assessments and actively discussed how to respond to students who had not yet learned. The thinking they had shared about how to alter their instruction now swirled into a dull film awaiting new ideas.

"Content. Contributor. Contaminant," he said.

She moved the marker along the smooth surface, automatically forming each *C* while she searched for what to say next. "Contaminant," she said.

"Yes," he said. "A rummy."

Turning to face him, she reminded herself to find the same practiced patience she had once used in her own classroom. He did not return her gaze.

"And how will regrouping the children by behavior help them learn?" she said.

"It won't," he said. "But I'll only have to deal with the rummies once a week."

Her grip tightened on the marker, and she was certain that his words had cut her. She turned to the whiteboard and pressed the black tip against it.

"What is another way you can think of to regroup the children that will help them learn?" she said, forcing a smile.

In this manner, the issue was decided.

TWO
Quick Spring

by Margot Fortunato Galt

The ditches are flowing on Highway 11
along the border with Canada.
The sky lifts immense skirts
into the bowl of heaven.

Raymond has written a poem
His class is gifted in poetry
but Raymond, absent the first day,
has put a white horse
    String-tailed
    Galloping glory
    Winter sufferer
    Non-meat eater
    Hay chomper
    Baby maker
    Friendly creature
on the page. He writes
    You
      You
        You
    Come back soon.

City-dweller, smart with words,
I ask,
    Did the horse bolt its traces?

It died, he says.

Raymond's teachers
can't quite believe
Raymond the LD,
whose older brothers
quit school, who lost his
favorite brother to a farm
accident and hasn't
been the same since,
Raymond with no
social graces
who can't read his own poem,
Raymond wrote what?

The best in the class, I hug
the paper to my breast.

Tell him, they insist, tell him.
Maybe he'll stay in school.

For a moment, their faces radiant
they forget how hard it can be,
like the drying crust of winter
a sky rife with snow
a white horse, its outline
edging into oblivion
    sway-backed,
    head-tossed yet
    still sweet,
    still visible
among a thousand
swirling words.

THREE

Artifacts

by Mary Harwell Sayler

In school, I learned
of wars and dates
that celebrate
the conqueror's pride
in victory.
It took me many
years to ask—
to take to task
the conquering side
of plot and story.
Why hide from me
the tapestry
of history
unfolding lots
of peoples, places,
homes?
Let's celebrate
the victory
of cooking pots
and combs.

FOUR

out of the mouths of scholars

by Kindel Nash

what really matters anyway?
that i would observe the decay
and decadence around me,
i mean the
degeneration of our world
flowing like a waterfall
out of the mouths of scholars.
scholars who say
kids who don't learn
1,200 words by pre-k
are doomed to fail in school,
something so wrong
i can feel it in my bones
and in the quickening of
my heartbeat.
scholars are like politicians
writing about the
objectification of mankind
with a stolen pen
on specially made paper
from some sweatshop.

what really matters anyway?
that i would be silent
when i feel my heart

begin to race,
when i could speak up!
yes, speak up like a
tiny white ant
screaming in the
most polite way
to a world of giants
that i could, that i have,
that i can,
observe
"such glaring racial disparities"
is such a privilege.
maybe i should just shut up.
constantly seeking approval,
redemption, solace,
observing, noticing, writing it down.
it's as empty as
a road studded with
abandoned warehouses,
a church with no roof
kids walking through the rubble

what really matters anyway?
i keep trying to find hope in my work
hope in a book
hope in the words of
scholars
while
the money flows
to those who will spout
"research" about
"those disadvantaged kids"
and the masses gather
'round racist panaceas
festering like
so many ants.
and what i don't know,
and what i can't tell them
is what really matters,
is the truth
that's already there.

FIVE

Dots, Lines, Spaces, and Math

by Geetha Durairajan

I am not a teacher of mathematics but have taught enough cousins in my school days the basics of percentages, time and distance, time and work, stocks and shares. But what I am writing about now is not that kind of teaching in which concepts may or may not get cleared. Instead I am writing about mathematics in everyday life: the mathematics that we see on the streets but do not bring into our classrooms, the sense of numbers and space that we have all around us. I am writing about two people who were part of my life more than thirty-five years ago.

The first is an "illiterate" milkman by the name Rangan; I have no clue whether he is still alive; chances are he is not. He was an inveterate drunkard and often had to be woken up from his stupor in the middle of the afternoon to relieve the udder-full cows of their milk. This drunkenness notwithstanding, Rangan was amazing. He had never been to school and did not know how to hold a pencil. Yet, that hand could cajole the most recalcitrant cow to yield milk.

But this was not all. The hand that could milk cows but could not "count" never made a mistake with calculations regarding the amount of milk that had to be supplied to people in ten houses. A piece of coal was all he used in those days to mark the milk he had given; a wall was his account book. The woman of the house would have to open her diary, add up all the halves, quarters, one and two liters, to arrive at the total amount of milk that she had bought. But such "counting" was not for

13

Rangan; his eye would at one glance take in the long and short and not-so-long lines, the different strokes that only he could decipher, and out would come the total. Not once did he make a mistake; fifteen minutes after he had "pronounced" the amount, the *amma* of the house would give him the figure, and there was never a discrepancy. But Rangan had never been to school, did not know how to read or write, was branded illiterate.

The second person is a lovely woman who has passed away by the grand name Pattu. She, too, did not know how to read or write and had, in her own words, "never stepped across the threshold of a school!" But if you gave Pattu a canvas, such as the front courtyard of your house, you were in for a visual feast! First, she would look at the spaces she had and, in the blink of an eye, the estimate would come: "*Amma*, grind two *azhaakkus* of rice!" This would happen one day before the festival. This ground rice, on festive occasions, and rice powder on ordinary days was her medium.

And then, the day of the kolam creations would dawn; Pattu would turn up either early in the morning, if it was a powder kolam, or the afternoon of the day before the festival, if it was a ground-rice kolam, and then her work would begin. It was a fantastic treat to watch her at work; not schooled, never using a protractor or compass or scale, but her kolams always had perspective. Small, medium, or large spaces; narrow, broad, rectangular, square, odd shaped, none of this mattered. Her eye would measure the space and, in accordance with availability, the spaces between the dots would increase or decrease; alternatively, she would choose bigger and more appropriate kolams.

This choice never came out of a book but from inside her head. A chariot, a peacock, kolams that had dots and lines, and kolams that had only intersecting lines; you name it, and she had the designs in her head. She might have passed away, but when I reflect, I can only look and wonder about how that unlettered head could carry all that information, how that eye could judge space and size so aptly.

Today, if we want to reduce or enlarge a diagram, we go to the photocopier, select the percentage, check, and by trial and error get it right. Pattu had an innate reducer/enlarger in her head. The eye glanced, and the hand did. I have spent hours watching the speed and grace with which she worked her magic on courtyards and floors to create these amazing pieces of art, art that got washed out and wiped clean and not preserved, but dexterity, imagination, skill, and talent it definitely exhibited.

Yet, being unlettered, no school would have allowed her admittance.

I am reminded of the grouch that the students of the Barbiana School have: that they failed in their gymnastics examination because they could not play basketball. But any one of the children in that school (an unconventional one run by an Italian priest for school dropouts) could climb an oak tree, let go with their hands, and chop off a two-hundred-pound branch with a hatchet and then drag it through the snow to their mother's doorstep. But these children will never get an *A* in gymnastics, just as Pattu and Rangan will never get an *A* in mathematics.

SIX
Taco Night

by Paul C. Gorski

I remember the invitations: red text on a white background, the name of the event in curly boldface surrounded by a crudely drawn piñata, a floppy sombrero, and a dancing cucaracha. A fourth-grader that year, I gushed with enthusiasm about these sorts of cultural festivals: the different, the alien, the other dancing around me, a dash of spice for a child of white-flighters. Ms. Manning distributed the invitations in mid-April, providing parents ample time to plan for the event, which occurred the first week of May, on or around Cinco de Mayo.

A few weeks later, my parents and I, along with a couple hundred other parents, teachers, students, and administrators, crowded into the cafeteria for Guilford Elementary School's annual Taco Night. The occasion was festive. I stared at the colorful decorations, like the papier-mâché piñatas designed by each fifth-grade class, then watched my parents try to squeeze themselves into cafeteria-style tables built for eight-year-olds. Sometimes the school hired a Mexican song-and-dance troupe from a neighboring town. They'd swing and sway and sing and smile, and I'd watch, bouncing dutifully to the rhythm, hoping they'd play "*La Bamba*" or "*Oye Como Va*" so I could sing along, pretending to know the words. If it happened to be somebody's birthday, the music teacher would lead us in a lively performance of "*Cumpleaños Feliz*" and give the kid some vaguely Mexican treats.

¡Olé!

17

Granted, not a single Mexican or Mexican American student attended Guilford at the time. However, I do recall Ms. Manning asking Adolfo, a classmate whose family had emigrated from Guatemala, whether the Taco Night tacos were "authentic." He answered with a shrug. Granted, too, there was little educational substance to the evening; I knew scarcely more about Mexico or Mexican American people upon leaving Taco Night than I did upon arriving. And granted, we never, in all my grade-school years, discussed more important concerns like, say, racism faced by Mexican Americans or the long, sordid history of US imperialist intervention throughout Latin America.

Still, hidden within Taco Night and the simultaneous absence of meaningful curricular attention to the lives, experiences, and histories of Mexicans, Mexican Americans, Chicanos, and other Latinos were three critical and clarifying lessons: (1) Mexican culture is synonymous with tacos; (2) *Mexican* and *Guatemalan* are synonymous, and by extension all Latino people are the same, and by further extension all Latino people are synonymous with tacos (as well as sombreros and dancing cucarachas); and (3) white people love tacos, especially in those hard, crunchy shells, which, I learned later, nobody in Mexico eats.

Thus began my diversity education—my introduction to a clearly identifiable "other." And I could hardly wait until Pizza Night.

SEVEN

Reflection Questions for Part One: Troubling Common Sense

1. The writers in this section challenge some of the common misperceptions people have about the current state of education, education reform initiatives, and teaching. What are some of these misperceptions? How might they derail attempts to create more equitable and just schools?
2. In "Artifacts," Mary Harwell Sayler challenges traditional approaches to teaching history. What are some of the concerns she raises in her poem? What does she mean by celebrating the "victory / of cooking pots / and combs"?
3. Paul C. Gorski's "Taco Night" challenges us to think more complexly as we try to implement diversity-related learning activities and curriculums. What are some of the issues he's encouraging us to consider?

Part Two

Revealing the Cost of Educational Tyranny

EIGHT

EDU Haiku

by Mari Ann Roberts

Testing overload
Small brown kids with no recess
Racing to the top

NINE

Standardized

by Alison Stone

Headaches, nausea, asthma, crying,
sleep disturbances, reluctance
to go to school—in forty-five states,
the children ready their pencils.
Let's Solve This, the Exxon announcer
purrs, while bright, hopeful cities
configure themselves in the background.
Using your knowledge
of oil companies, what can you infer
about the speaker's motives? How is Common Core
like drilling in the sea?

* * *

There were three pages of instructions, which teachers
were required to read verbatim, including
Are there any questions
on how to darken the circles?

One of my third graders started hyperventilating,
coughing, and turned red. The TA walked him out. He stayed
with the nurse for 15 minutes before returning to finish the test.

Most of the class ran out of time. Many never got to the essay. The teacher
had to pry the test from one kid's hand. He kept writing and crying
until the teacher took the paper away.

The multiple choice questions frequently had two equally valid choices.

The 6th and 8th grade tests are taken from text books sold by Pearson.
What level of advantage does this give districts who choose/can afford
to purchase these books?

* * *

The same questions occur in tests for grades 3, 4, and 5.
This is not an error.
Vertical linking will help prepare questions for next year's tests.

* * *

Which paragraph best illustrates the theme in paragraph 2?
Paragraph 4, paragraph 9, paragraph 3, or paragraph 11?

One multiple choice math problem had no correct answer.

Two middle school boys wet their pants.
This is not an error.
Students need to be *college-ready and able to compete in a global economy.*
One child vomited on the test,
which was wiped off and collected *for security reasons.*

Studies show toxic stress interferes with brain functioning and can result in
the formation of a smaller brain.

* * *

An ELA passage which occurred in tests around the country tells the story of the
Pineapple and the Hare. The pineapple challenges the hare to a race to prove
which animal is the fastest. *You aren't even an animal! You're a tropical fruit!* But the
hare agrees. All the animals predict victory for the hare until the crow asserts that
the pineapple, knowing he cannot move, must have a trick up his sleeve. Wanting
to back a winner, the other animals cheer for the pineapple. The race begins—the
hare takes off, and the pineapple remains stationary. A few hours later the hare
crosses the finish line. The animals eat the pineapple.

Moral: Pineapples Don't Have Sleeves

The animals ate the pineapple because they were

hungry
excited
annoyed
amused

This is not an error.
The standards are designed to be robust and relevant to the real world.

If 100 percent of Commissioner King's children attend a private Montessori school that rejects standardized testing and the Common Core, write a sample budget reallocating the 350 million dollars spent on developing new tests toward programs such as art, music, language immersion, and resources such as air conditioning, clean drinking water, and healthy low-cost lunch. Show your work.

TEN
Act V

by Kelly Jean Olivas

We will not have died hereafter
Before a time for silenced words.

Test, after test, after test
Crept on from petty to proficient
To the last lame window of kidnapped time;
And all your multiple non-choices left childhood behind
as you raced to the bottom. Out, out, tragic fools!
Kids are not captive shadows led by data-driven drones
To find only "correct" answers
And never discover real ones. Yours was just another tale
Told by but not to idiots, full of profit yet no promise
And reforming nothing.

ELEVEN

a lesson from an elementary principal

by Korina Jocson

A version of this poem first appeared in E. Lozada, ed., 2008, *Field of Mirrors: An Anthology of Philippine American Writers*, San Francisco: PAWA, 57.

in school
i never use
wooden rulers
for art class
their edges
remind me
of lined scars
on my knuckles
marks
since age five
disfigured
cursive letters
insist
to heal
tremble
sometimes
just to write
my name

TWELVE

Phoenixes

by Julia Stein

Sweet students, you sit in your sweaters and jackets
this Southcentral classroom with no heat when
the temperature's near freezing, and school has cut classes.
The medical students call this place the war zone —
emergency rooms full of young men with
gunshot wounds from gang killings.

Sweet students, I've complained three times;
nobody fixes the heat. The tile in the hall is
falling down — more empty holes than ceiling.
Students keep walking in this first day until no more
chairs. One male student borrows them from other rooms.
I don't have an office to meet you after class.

Sweet students, I want my classroom always
to have heat sizzling, all of you to have enough chairs
so we can all sit down, want a wooden desk in an
office with a swivel metal chair, and all the cut classes
like phoenixes reborn. I want us to sit surrounded by
phoenixes of reborn classes in cozily warm classrooms

THIRTEEN

This Thing of Memory

by Andrena Zawinski

This poem first appeared in A. Zawinski, 1995, *Traveling in Reflected Light*, Youngstown, OH: Pig Iron Press.

I was teaching my students today to write
letters, coaxing children to daydream,
to retrieve some small scrap of thought
we call memory: to let it grow into a poem,
like the big wide of a smile only littlest ones
get away with, the kind that freezes thin
on the front room stiff of adult faces.

Their heads bowed to their desks, eyes
forced shut by the mesmerizing drum
and roll of my voice, they walked, skipped,
spun in sun and rain and snow, watched
pictures pass beneath their lids, gathered touch
at the fingertips before—like so many other
little things—they might quickly slip away.

And I wrote with them and read to them
of how I put white clay ducks on my grandmother's
grassy yard that summer of unparched green
in the space where fat-headed sunflowers pressed
through a patch of slate toward sky, and how she
told me then when once she was a girl she had
real ducks somewhere faraway in a place called Poland.

And the children read what they wrote:
a boy danced in abandon with his grandfather
across the kitchen floor, a girl held on tight
to the perfumed soft of her new mother's arms.
But when I asked one—so slight it seemed she

could be carried off by wind—why tears fell
onto the page ending a day feeding cows,
she said the word: nothing. In my chest
the panic of a whole city of doors slammed
shut to keep out impending dark.

At my brother's house later that afternoon,
where I went to witness the magic of a new
baby born into the room, I asked him for the ducks,
the ones whose pink eyes our own grandmother
wiped clear from dust with her apron corner.
He snapped they were long gone, and chickens anyway.

In my marvel and belief in the magical accuracy
of memory, I shuffled through the tattered
edged packet of yellowed pictures—as if to cast
some fortune teller's proof of it, of her, of me,
the ducks—and there they were: chickens.

I wonder now about this thing of memory:
how as it clouds up we can heave back
with an angler's veracity, the fish story grown
too large to lift; how a small child will reel it in
fresh, but when asked, Why are you crying?
as if to raise a talisman of real against the past,
postured in a distance forged by remembering,
can say, as a matter of fact: Oh, it's nothing.

FOURTEEN

Answering the Call

by Jeff McCullers

Their bags are stowed, and all eyes are forward:
I take my place at the appointed time,
Recording precisely who is present
And who has failed to report for learning.

I state the standard for today's lesson,
Noting the domain and topic cluster;
Observing the attention of children
Gathered here so that I can add value.

I read the script, and I show the symbols,
They repeat the words and they make the marks.
The objectives met, the lesson concluded,
So we await the signal to change rooms.

I notice our proud achievement rosters
Taped up so to cover the small window
Have curled open at a corner or two
Leaving a gap through which the sunlight streams.

The girl in row six, desk four also sees:
I catch her peering at a bird outside.
This is my summons to do what is right,
This glimpsed little bird now calls me to teach.

At the tone, the children leave with their bags
While I answer the bird's call to duty:

I tape closed the gap; I shut out the light:
A good teacher must maintain high standards.

FIFTEEN

The Auspices of Social Justice

by Shannon Audley-Piotrowski

I entered teaching, like many young, enthusiastic, privileged students, through magic. One day I was an undergraduate student, finishing my degree in biology with no plans for the future except to change the world, and the next day, poof, I was a teacher, in charge of lives that I could tangibly change. I heard from friends that schools were failing and subsequently needed teachers who were willing to make a difference. Children in urban cities were caught in the cycle of poverty because certified teachers were not willing to work hard enough to make a difference; future generations were at risk because their teachers lacked enthusiasm to make science content dance. As a child who had grown up grounded in middle-class values, I knew that education was the vehicle for this type of progress. If children needed a cheerleader to fuel their path toward success, I would willingly sacrifice a couple of years of my life for them.

I applied to two programs, Educators for America (EFA) and New Catholic Educators (NCE), that I decided would help facilitate the difference I was going to make and was accepted at both. The first program, EFA, offered six weeks of training in the summer but offered no subsequent training for the remaining two-year commitment. More worrisome to me, however, was that the teacher support system in the area was weak at the time, and the local colleges near my tentative placement site did not offer graduate education in my teaching area. I would be making a difference, yes, but I would not be moving my own education forward.

Yet, I still lovingly and carefully considered the program; they beguiled me with e-mails about what I would do once the program was over, explaining how I would be connected to a wider network that would offer many opportunities inside and outside of the classroom and education. I even started receiving e-mails from prestigious graduate schools that offered to delay my enrollment if I enrolled in this prestigious teacher program. It did not seem to matter, then, that I would start my teaching career with six weeks of training, as I would be moving into other greener pastures at the end of my commitment.

The second program, NCE, was similar in its program structure to EFA in that it also offered six weeks of summer teacher training. In addition to this training, we would also be taking four graduate-level education courses with other master's degree students both summers and three education courses during the school year while we taught. After two years' commitment, we would have completed the required coursework for teacher certification and a master's degree. Because I planned on enrolling in graduate school in the sciences after the program anyway, I thought having an M.Ed. would increase my desirability and competitiveness as a candidate for a prestigious graduate program. In the end, on my father's advice, I decided to exchange teaching in urban schools for a master's degree in education. He warned me, though, that teaching was not as easy as it looked. He looked me gently in the eye and told me I was making the "best" choice of my self-imposed, limited options; neither choice would really change my students' lives, only my own.

My father was a teacher, so I had a rough idea of what teachers did. He taught for twenty-seven years, spending the first part of his career in an elementary school that served an immigrant population, and he finished his career coordinating a GED program at a boys' ranch for juvenile delinquents. I was told later that he was quite effective at what he did and was even recognized for his work with an award. He taught his students to read and write and to pass the GED. When he saw them on the street or when he would go to the restaurants where they invariably worked, his former students would greet him and let him know that they were still on track, always looking him in the eye and shaking his hand with pride, telling him that they were doing their best to make him proud. His "successful" students weren't college bound; they weren't moving mountains to make the world a better place. They often didn't change their social or economic status. It never occurred to me to ask why his successful students were waiters or movie ticket takers, bartenders, or small joint cooks. My father found teaching a worthy profession, and that was enough. So why did I see it as a stepping stone to something else?

I arrived in Memphis early in June, just a few weeks after college graduation, and met the others who, like me, had been called to serve to make a difference and to give back. Only one student in our cohort had majored in education, and she ended up being the first to quit the program at the beginning of August. Everyone else, like me, had sacrificed something because he or she wanted to make a difference. Alice had given up her boyfriend in Alabama. Tran was doing service to build her resume for medical school. Michael left an unfulfilling career at a logistics company and his parents' house. I had put on hold a lucrative career in the sciences. At least that is what I told myself. Within a few days of arriving, graduate school started, and we began taking classes. Only a few months past graduation, and with only a summer session of grad school under our belts, we were given our teaching assignments.

By January, six of the thirteen original members of our cohort left the program and their schools, all but one because of the pressure they felt from the daunting task of teaching unprepared in some of the most impoverished neighborhoods in the country. Another left the following summer, and only six of us remained by the start of the second school year and through to the end of the program. Change wasn't supposed to be this hard, especially for high-achieving and enthusiastic individuals. I started to think that maybe the problem in education wasn't that teachers weren't trying hard enough.

Although I was a middle school teacher, the principal asked me to take over teaching the high school science courses that were abandoned by a teacher who quit the program. I took over a series of science classes where the pace had been robust but manageable. I took the class over with zeal, trying to convince them that I would not quit. They were concerned that I would leave, and that was the last thing they wanted. They wanted to know what they had to do to be successful because they had college ambitions, and they wanted to know how to get through, how to navigate the sciences and feel successful. They were worried that I would leave, that I wasn't going to invest in them just as the previous teacher had not. We spent the rest of the semester in a gray zone; they did what I asked, mostly, but they were at times doubtful. Would it really matter if they turned in their homework? It would matter if I was choosing students to be in my honors chemistry class next year, but would I be teaching honors chemistry next year? Should they study harder? They would if they knew that I was going to be teaching an AP chemistry course. But they were not sure, so they were inconsistent, and rightfully so. They joked at the end of the year that they would sign up for physics if I promised to teach it the following year. Why wouldn't I? I replied. I can't wait, I would tell them.

And yet, I knew that I would leave. The program that helped me make a difference was structured so I could make a difference for two years and then continue my own path. I would leave even though I was the most qualified to stay and make a difference after earning a master's degree in education. I would leave even though I was more invested in the students' lives and knowledgeable about what they needed to know and how I needed to teach them. We would have worked together toward success, but in order for the program to grow and make the difference it was intended to make, I needed to leave and move on so another idealistic person could come into my place and struggle as I struggled in the first year. It would be someone else's turn to make the difference. Somehow, this did not seem right to me. I had done the hard work of getting to know them, and the students were making progress.

The content of each class and my dedication to pedagogy may have improved my students' ACT scores, but my enthusiasm didn't change the fact that Sherice had to work a job after school to help her family earn a living or that Kayte had to watch her brothers after school so their mom could work a night shift. All the enthusiasm and content knowledge in the world wouldn't change the obstacles that my students faced. How does one continue to stress the importance of learning, standards, testing, and content when that kind of success won't change the students' personal struggles? All the enthusiasm in the world couldn't give Sherice more time to complete her homework or Kayte a break from watching her siblings.

In the second year, I was starting to feel settled. I had developed a reputation among the students that suited me. I was more confident. I had many of my students again. There were four students, Kim, Kobe, Xander, and Brad, who excelled in honors chemistry and followed me into physics. Neilson was in my biology class again, and it wasn't until the second time I had him that I realized he failed because he couldn't read. Arlando was in my biology class again, too, and I also taught him summer school English and remedial math. I helped arrange for a special diploma for Arlando, as he had extreme learning differences that had gone undiagnosed. Although both Arlando and Neilson had failed my class previously, they spent their free periods in my class, helping me set up chemistry experiments for a class that they would never be allowed to attend. It didn't matter. They didn't fault me for that, and I appreciated their help and getting to know them. I felt comfortable with my less-than-idealistic role. I was also beginning to feel more comfortable in the other roles I played in the community. When I coached the softball team to yet another loss, I joked with the parents that I was better at calculating how far a hit would go than helping a player catch the ball, and sometimes we talked about next season, and how next year we might win a game.

In the spring of my second year, Kim asked if I could teach an AP chemistry course. Kim was in my physics class and had taken honors chemistry her sophomore year as well. She was a gifted student from Mississippi. She rose at 5 a.m. to catch a forty-minute bus ride to school every day because her family could not afford the gas to drive her to school. She told me that Kobe, Xander, and Brad would sign up as well, and she could get more students if necessary. She told me she would work all summer to pay for the gas and that she would come in on weekends to make sure that they could stay ahead. I knew that she would. She was a star student, and I knew I was lucky to have had her in my first year teaching and again in my second. I would be even luckier to have her for a third year. I had just received a college chemistry book in the mail, one that would be perfect for an advanced placement chemistry course, and I thought to myself, I could stay another year, I could teach the AP chemistry class, I could see Kim, Kobe, Xander, and Brad graduate and go to college, but in the end, I did not. The program was two years, and my two years were up.

I went into teaching to make a difference. What I failed to realize then, and did not realize for many years, was that the difference I made was in myself. I didn't really make a difference in the students' lives beyond teaching them science content, at least not in the ways that I had initially intended. I wish I could say that Kim went to a great college and graduated at the top of her class, but she didn't. She went to a local college and dropped out after two years. No matter how hard I worked, my teaching could not change the fact that she came from a background that made it difficult to be successful in a way that is defined by the middle class and in the way that I had set out to do.

More so, I thought my role as their teacher ended once they had learned the content. I failed to realize the impact I had on the students with the most need. Unlike my father, who went to the places where his former students worked and saw them in their highs and lows, I do not know for sure what happened to Kobe or Brad or Xander. I don't know whether Arlando graduated or if Neilson ever learned to read. I do not know what colleges Kayte applied to or whether she was accepted because I did not help her get there; not really. I bought into the idea of teaching as a way to make a difference because it made me feel better but not of education as social justice. I had not stopped to think about why my students deserved an education.

Growing up middle class, I often wondered why my dad took us to restaurants where his students worked. These places were outside of our comfort zone. Both his students and the other patrons greeted my dad. He may have lived outside of that community, but he made it a point to understand and be a part of that community, and this made all the difference in the world. I failed in my quest for justice because I did not consider the whole picture of my students: where they came from and where they wanted to go. I did not consider their past, and I could visualize their future only through my own eyes, not theirs. I taught them in the present, for the present, because that is where I could see my difference being made.

I did go back to graduate school but in educational psychology, not the sciences, and now I teach in an education department at a liberal arts college. Every semester I counsel students who aim to enter a program like I did to "make a difference" before they start their "real careers." They expect me to be an immediate ally in their desire to make a difference. I am, at best, a reluctant ally. I saw education as the vehicle for progress, but it was my own progress that prevailed, not the students' that I taught. I hope that my bright, enthusiastic undergraduates will take the time to reflect about what it really means to follow the call to teach for greater equality and social justice. I fear that they are enamored with the sudden magic of knowing one's place in the world and being provided with a structured sequential path for success under the acceptable guise of making a difference. I fret every day that they will follow that path, my path, and pad their own resumes on the auspices of social justice.

SIXTEEN

Reflection Questions for Part Two: Revealing the Cost of Educational Tyranny

1. Several of the stories and poems in this section shine a critical light on the increasing reliance on high-stakes testing in public education. What are some of the troublesome implications of this increasing reliance explored by the contributors?

2. In "Answering the Call," Jeff McCullers bemoans the impacts of standardization and scripted teaching and learning on his teaching and his students' engagement. How can we, as educators, manage the very real pressures of these conditions while continuing to engage students in deep ways?

3. In her poem "Act V," Kelly Jean Olivas refers to a variety of school reform initiatives as "another tale . . . full of profit yet no promise." What does she mean by "profit"? Who "profits" from today's school reform initiatives?

Part Three

Honoring Liberated Voices

SEVENTEEN

I Apologize

by Alejandro Jimenez

When I was in 3rd grade
At least three times a week
I would come home with my pants wet

from my own pee.

See, Mrs. Parrot
Wouldn't allow me to use the bathroom
Because I wasn't pronouncing
My request correctly

Blame it on these cheek bones, Mrs. Parrot
On this bent out of shape jaw
Passed down to me by martyrs
It holds secrets I wish I could understand

Many times I've wanted to stop its clenching
But my mouth is like my people
We do not deal well with assimilation
Or systems of oppression

Despite the bibles shoved to the bottom of my stomach
The paper cuts on my gums
Can tell you what we have been through

Lynching
Doesn't just happen by the neck, Mrs. Parrot

My tongue
Was treated like Emmett Till
Beaten
Strangled
Thrown into the bottom of Lago Texcoco

Hanged like Joaquin Murrieta
Decapitated and displaced

Cut off like braids upon arrival to boarding schools

Stretched in four directions like Túpac Amaru until he ripped

So I apologize for my mispronunciation
If I made you point your ear toward my mouth
I am sorry
I never meant to make you waste your energy

But I have bodies
Suspended from my vocal cords
Their dangling feet
Scratch the base of my throat
So I apologize if I stutter

Mrs. Parrot,

There are memories of conquistadors feeding babies to dogs
Buried inside of my tongue
I wish I couldn't remember them
That's why sometimes you have to ask me to repeat myself
Because my brother's stomach, empty, grumbling
From searching for food in Tijuana dumpsters at the age of 2
After being deported with my mother
Did not wash down my saliva enough
To have your words roll off the tip of my tongue flawlessly

I apologize Mrs. Parrot
Because my native language refuses to die
Because there are temples planted on top of my teeth
That's why they are called wisdom
And that's why I won't go to the dentist
Because they will try to pull it out

Because like the blankets you gave us
I have smallpox for taste buds
And they get in my way when I try to speak
So I apologize for mumbling

My annunciation is not the best, Mrs. Parrot

Because Mesa Verde was carved into
The inner walls of my cheeks
Long before its current place

I could show you

But you wouldn't understand
Just like you don't understand
Why it is that I keep quiet sometimes

It's because I have Sitting Bull's headdress hanging
From the roof of my mouth
And I am afraid you may want to steal it just like you did his Black Hills

I apologize if my lips are too stiff
To shape your words correctly, Mrs. Parrot
They are still dry from our desert walk to get to this country

Mrs. Parrot!
Did you advise my current employers to send me to speech classes?
Did you ever imagine how I explained to my mother that I peed my pants?
Again,
    Again,
        And again?

Mrs. Parrot,
I really, really
need
to go

I have been holding this for such a long time
I need to let it out

It may smell like genocide
Like burnt ancient scriptures

But you told me to pronounce my words correctly
And for me that means to speak the truth

As proof that I have mastered your language
I wrote you this note
So, Mrs. Parrot:
May I please go to the bathroom?

EIGHTEEN

Seeds

by Mayra Evangelista

Wait, hold on
so you want to tell me racism no longer exists?
Or is it that there's an invisible Jim Crow?
Okay so explain to me this: why is it that my culture
mi gente
aren't in these history books?
How do you think we feel when our legacy has been erased?
Oh but then you show me there we are on page 1492;
we are the hostiles, the bandits, we are the villains.
Why is it that I'm learning about
the grand success of Colonel John Chivington
portrayed as a war hero instead of the man who
massacred our families at Sand Creek
who took fetuses and body parts as battle trophies.
So is this how we leave our natives behind?
When I bring light to this
it's automatically, "No honey you're wrong."

What's wrong is the fact that I can't go to the mall
without you following me around the store
like some kind of suspect
the same way the police patrols my brothers
with their brown dickies backpacks

500 years of racism embedded in our institutions.
Conditioned to believe our colored skin to be of less worth.

Conditioned to assume dark skin is "bad."
Conditioned to believe equality means living in a colorblind society.

My brown woman's culture is not a white woman's accessory.

Don't you worry though
mi papa me enseño
que no nomas soy princesa pero también Adelita.
Soldadera de mi comunidad.
Just like my ancestors said
"They tried burying us, they didn't know we were seeds."
My roots are intact
siempre será nuestra tierra
you can never colonize our spirit.

NINETEEN
A Classroom Assignment

by María Gabriel

We were having
a debate—
about illegal immigrants.

Some chick
gave a speech—
about immigration.
Everyone started
arguing about it.

We were
having a discussion—
about the American culture.
People always
bring Mexicans into it . . .

Stereotyping Mexicans,
Putting Mexicans into
these little categories—
Labeling us.

You know,
we're not
the *only* immigrants
in the United States.

This data poem "A Classroom Assignment" was created out of lines from the transcripts of my 2011 dissertation study about how students perceive the classroom environment to become a hostile learning environment as the topic of immigration causes them to be marginalized. It emphasizes the need for educators to be conscious of the implications of their instructional decisions as related to cultural identities.

TWENTY

"Where Are You From?"

by Hana Alhady

"Where are you from?" you ask me . . .
. . . searching for the answer
under my feet,
in my hair,
beneath my breath,
beyond my eyeballs,
trying to pull it out from the depth of my shaking bones,
sucking it out from my warm veins.

And when I scream out of pain,
you look at me surprised, smile and walk away.

TWENTY-ONE

Felipe

by Janice Sapigao

Every day after school
For two years
I sat at a chipped table
Making outlines, piecing textbook history,
Conjugating French verb tenses

Until it made sense
To college bound minds
Warmed inside hooded sweatshirts
Learning behind eyeliner and piercings
Thinking between earbuds of hip hop bars

Felipe walked by me
Every afternoon
With new stories
About how his homework
Didn't exist today

He always had time
To dap the distracted boys,
Straighten posture in front of girls
And leave sooner than I could
Ask him to stay

Felipe roamed the hallways—
Black backpack over one shoulder
A cool silhouette

That slipped behind the shadows
Of adults looking to help him

The only assignment
Felipe ever needed help with
Was an apology letter
To the cop who caught him
Jaywalking to tutoring

I told him, "The formula
To writing these things is simple:
Pretend,
What if you were him?
What would you want to read?"

"So I'm a sorry ass dude
with nothing better to do
than micro-police youth?
Then, this letter will be
Sweeter than the ones
I give to my teachers."

TWENTY-TWO

unpredicted storm

by Cathi LaMarche

veering from the path
the teacher invites questions
a windstorm ensues

TWENTY-THREE

Reflection Questions for Part Three: Honoring Liberated Voices

1. This section is comprised of poems in which people who have been marginalized in school unleash their voices and demand justice. In your view, which students are most marginalized in schools today? What are some of the ways in which those students are attempting to share their stories and demand change?

2. In "I Apologize," Alejandro Jimenez describes being silenced by his third-grade teacher. What are some of the conditions that silence him? How can we create classroom and school spaces where students do not feel silenced?

Part Four

Teaching Against the Grain

TWENTY-FOUR

Punk Has Always Been My School

by Rebekah Cordova and Erin Bowers

PUNK HAS ALWAYS BEEN MY SCHOOL

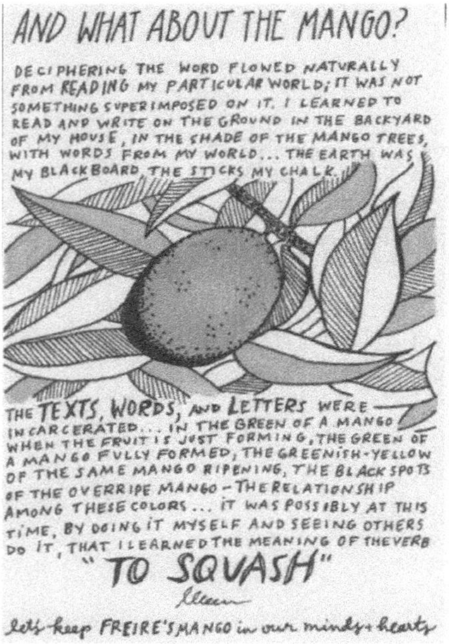
AND WHAT ABOUT THE MANGO?
DECIPHERING THE WORD FLOWED NATURALLY FROM READING MY PARTICULAR WORLD; IT WAS NOT SOMETHING SUPERIMPOSED ON IT. I LEARNED TO READ AND WRITE ON THE GROUND IN THE BACKYARD OF MY HOUSE, IN THE SHADE OF THE MANGO TREES, WITH WORDS FROM MY WORLD... THE EARTH WAS MY BLACKBOARD, THE STICKS MY CHALK.
THE TEXTS, WORDS, AND LETTERS WERE INCARCERATED... IN THE GREEN OF A MANGO WHEN THE FRUIT IS JUST FORMING, THE GREEN OF A MANGO FULLY FORMED, THE GREENISH-YELLOW OF THE SAME MANGO RIPENING, THE BLACK SPOTS OF THE OVERRIPE MANGO – THE RELATIONSHIP AMONG THESE COLORS... IT WAS POSSIBLY AT THIS TIME, BY DOING IT MYSELF AND SEEING OTHERS DO IT, THAT I LEARNED THE MEANING OF THE VERB
"TO SQUASH"
let's keep FREIRE'S MANGO in our minds + hearts

SO LET'S TALK MORE ABOUT LITERACY—AND LET'S BRING IT OUT FROM UNDERNEATH WHAT SOME OF OUR TEXTS ASSERT—AND INTO THE WAYS IN WHICH WE HAVE ALL FELT LITERATE IN OUR OWN LIVES. AND FOR THIS MOMENT, LET'S DEFINE LITERACY THE MOST PRIVATE WAYS WE CAN... IF YOU DON'T RESTRICT YOUR DEFINITION OF LITERACY TO READING TEXT OR SYMBOLS, HOW WOULD YOU DEFINE IT?
ART? SOME KIDS CAN BEST EXPRESS THEMSELVES THROUGH DRAWING OR PAINTING.
WOULD IT BE LIKE THE MULTIPLE INTELLIGENCES?
IF YOU FEEL LITERATE, YOU FEEL INTELLIGENT– YOU FEEL SMART.
YOU CAN NAVIGATE WITH MORE THAN WORDS– YOU KNOW, OTHER PARTS OF LIFE.

LET'S TALK ABOUT
Stories...
WE TELL OURSELVES STORIES IN ORDER TO LIVE. -JOAN DIDION

LET'S WRITE ON THIS TONIGHT– YOUR STORY OF FIRST LITERACY. IN OTHER WORDS, THINK BACK TO YOUR EARLIEST MEMORIES OF LITERACY. CAN YOU REMEMBER THAT VERY FIRST EVENT OR HAPPENING OR EXPERIENCE WHEN YOU FELT LITERATE?
TELL THAT STORY

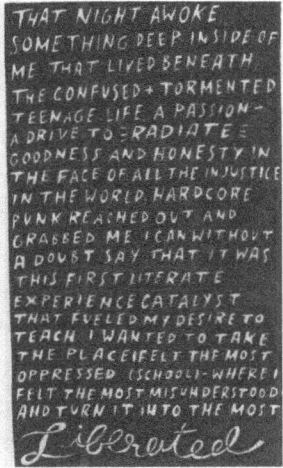

"You will see a conversation unfold in your classroom and schools - when you are face to face with a child who is learning how to read, how to de-code words - when students are attempting to make meaning of a text that you are presenting to them."
"And, perhaps, you will be told that the student should be able to read and comprehend said texts for a variety of reasons... because of how old they are... or because of the assessment results found in their files."
"But there will come a time, and my guess is that it will be soon enough—
that you will know deep down—that before the student can make the meaning
of these words, before there can be true internal comprehension
that the student will depend on their lived experience
to make sense of things
the student will
to find their own mango.
JAWBREAKER

TWENTY-FIVE

Pickled

by Sarah Warren

Trust is not a bloom
of scarlet flowering underneath

plastic adhesive where the needle
pulls test after test and sends

my students, dull-eyed dolls
with lids that open and close,

to nod mindlessly, sit pickled
in ringing silence with the threat

of contemplation. This
monotony of examination

is the air we breathe:
assimilated philosophy disguised

in assembly line production.
Measures and objectives.

They want to know
something real. I tell them:

I have a map of myself
and don't know how to read it.

I've seen no stars, though I've heard
the learned astronomer, and spent
every night outside looking up.

TWENTY-SIX

They Are Me and I Am Them: A Memoir of a Social Justice Educator

by Cherise Martinez-McBride

I run across the ABC carpet with as much speed as my four-year-old legs will allow. The glossy, bright-pink hardcover book I'm holding shines between my extended arms; I bear it proudly, like a giant package ready for delivery. My destination is clear; I'm making a beeline to the lady who comes to our Head Start class sometimes. Every time she comes, she listens to me read. She sits patiently in the roomy chair near the corner of our classroom. She is my Tía Lucy.

Her name rolls off my tongue with fondness now, although back then I didn't know her as my tía. We didn't spend Christmases together or have family reunions. I didn't see her much outside school. To me, like all the adults there, she was my teacher.

Tía Lucy smiles as I scramble into her lap and asks what I have there in my hands. I am the superstar. I proudly announce the familiar title. "Corduroy and the Lost Button," I read through the space where my two front teeth used to be. I open it and start recounting the familiar tale to her, settling once again into that place of comfort. I look up as I close the last page, and Tía Lucy's head is lying on the back of the cozy chair. She is still smiling. She opens her eyes when I stop talking.

"Wow. You read the whole book," she declares with enthusiasm. "I didn't know you could read like that, m'ija! You're so smart. How old are you now?"

"Four," I say.

"Wow, I've never seen a four-year-old who could read like you."

I basked in the light of that specialness. I didn't know how pivotal that year would be for me then. Now I realize it etched in my heart an assurance I never shook. I looked forward to that feeling every day when I crossed the threshold from the Clinton Avenue Housing Project to Funston Head Start just around the corner. Mama would walk me over, my sister in the fold-up stroller and me hopping alongside the two of them. I remember Mama would sign me in at the front desk, and I'd go off to join the other kids for breakfast. Bright mornings of singing, counting, and wondering what Brown Bear saw and where was Thumbkin slowly turned into calmer afternoons full of dozing and then reading like I did with my Tía Lucy.

Funston is where I first remember hearing that word *smart*. It became a word that meant I was special; it meant that I would be asked to help whenever the teacher needed it; it meant I'd be asked to do things no one else did, like read a book to the class during circle time. Soon, it meant awards and certificates. It meant that I was important. School was the place where *smart* mattered, so it became the place where I wanted to be.

As a teacher now, I can't help but wonder what it takes to create that same sensation in the students I teach. Even though my students are on the other end of the educational spectrum—in high school, adult school, and community college—I am certain that what happened for me in those early school experiences must happen for my students as well. The majority of the students I teach would be considered "at risk" by most measures. Because of their backgrounds and socioeconomics, they are statistically at risk for dropping out, being incarcerated, witnessing or perpetrating violence, and the list continues. Additionally, they have experienced gaps in their schooling due to truancy, illness, frequent moves, instability, and a host of other causes. In spite of these factors, they must meet the same academic demands as other students: earning a certain number of academic credits and passing benchmark exams. The pressure that exists in that conundrum is at times palpable.

It is Shanell running to and fro during her senior year of high school, working on extra projects, racking up service learning credits, attending study groups, and spending hours in the computer lab to type final drafts. She can almost see herself crossing that graduation stage, and she could be the first in her family to do so. Still, the pressure of passing her exit exam looms, and she wonders whether it's still worth trying.

It is Marla squeezing in time for my class at the adult school, using a tutor at the local library, and sacrificing to pay the $175 required to take the GED so that she can achieve more for her family. In her early thirties, she declares with clear distress, "I can't write an essay! I've never been good at school!" She's sure she's never been confident at tests, and the self-deprecating thoughts threaten to debilitate her.

It is Ricky following the advice of a guidance counselor and signing up for community college, only to discover that he has two English classes to take before any of his English credits will even be transferable. Meanwhile, growing financial pressure to meet his immediate needs makes him wonder whether this is really the path for him.

All of these students know pressure well—they know the pressure to perform in the moment. Deep down they question whether any of their efforts will make a difference: a difference toward achieving their goals; a difference concerning their tangible needs; and on a larger scale, a difference in their families, communities, and overall realities. As a student, I often wondered about these things. As I attended awards ceremonies alone; lost certificates in countless moves; and for a period, living without electricity, rushed to get all my homework done while it was still light outside, I, too, felt that pressure and wondered whether the effort was worth it all. My grandmother's persistent advice, "Focus on your education, and you'll be blessed," became my measure of faith.

As a teacher, I have seen the pressure in tearful test anxiety, misdirected anger, and empty seats. My students are well aware that some tests will be gatekeepers to their futures. The challenges can seem insurmountable, not only for them but also for me as an educator. In those moments, what fuels my teaching is the residue of that feeling I had back at Funston.

School is fun. School is safe. There is no yelling at school, only smiles and listening and stickers. I am a good reader. I am a superstar.

When I feel overwhelmed with the task at hand, when Ray refuses to take notes, Jalia is snapping at everyone who passes by, and I have to ask to speak to Davina after class yet again, I pause. I remember that, in my classroom, I am the architect. I map out curriculum, design seating charts, and arrange desks in ways that facilitate learning. And once the foundation is built, I am also the thermostat. Like so many of my former teachers, I decide that I will be consistent and keep our environment warm and safe for learning. I recognize that school for me was a place of security and praise, but for many of my students it is at best a place of challenge and at worst one of consistent failure and possibly ridicule. Aware of the odds they face, the baggage they bring, and the urgency of their education, I make it my job to bring their strengths, their points of celebration, to the surface. All students deserve the spotlight.

At the start of every course, I have each student write a letter to me in response to one I have written to each of them. Sometimes I use Linda Christensen's "Where I'm From" poem assignment. Through these assignments, I gain just enough to let them know that I see them; I know they're there. Their presence matters. I offer my observations directly: "I notice that you have been on time every day this week." "Jake, how did your MMA match go last night?" "Those of us who have children may enjoy this article," I might say with a nod to my fellow parents in the room. As I teach content, I also make room for connection. It is never too late for student-centered curriculum.

From that place, it becomes permissible, even natural, to hold high expectations for all students. On the basis of trust and commitment, they will rise to meet the expectations I set. To this day, I'm not even sure whether I was actually reading the words of *Corduroy* or if I'd only memorized the story. But somehow, much as it would in the future, the safety and attention compelled me to keep trying, to do what others knew I could do. In seventh-grade geography Mr. Faggionato would require us to know and label every country in the world. Fortunately we did it in spurts, ten or so countries at a time, and each red smiley on the quizzes made me a little more confident. In tenth-grade AP US history, Mr. Ikeda graded us hard and took no excuses on our DBQs. In math, Mr. Smith gave As sparingly, making sure that, when we received them, we *knew* we earned them. And as I said goodbye to high school, Mrs. Markovich wrote in my yearbook, "Let me know when you get your doctorate." I didn't even know what that was, but I knew that, if she thought I could do it, there must be some truth there that I simply had yet to discover.

Along with building relationships and setting high expectations, I make it a point to make the classroom predictable. We have routines, a clear objective on the board, an agenda, and some nonnegotiable norms. Looking back, in my four-year-old sphere, there was so much I couldn't control: I knew that Mama was hurt and angry and that something in the letters she read from Daddy made her cry. I knew it would be a very long time before we saw Daddy again. I learned that my questions and even my tears wouldn't bring him home. I knew that, no matter how loudly I talked or clapped or sang, my little sister couldn't hear me. (We later learned that she was deaf.) I knew that some things, like how much food was in our refrigerator or who came over yesterday, were things for only us to know, things that even Grandma and Paw-Paw didn't need to find out. Alongside these truths, I continued to experience school as a safe place. It was the same every day. Teachers smiled, friends invited me to play, and there were always, always snacks.

Now I am the mother of a four-year-old. Like me, she loves pink, prefers chocolate to vanilla, and already hates to miss school. Like me, she's a big sister who thrives on structure but has a silly streak that makes her laugh powerfully. Like me, she asks incessant questions and reacts in gleeful surprise when she makes a new discovery. Yet as much as we are alike in our caramel skin, detailed observations, and self-proclaimed familial leadership, our lives will be—indeed already are—quite different.

She knows her Daddy loves her Mama and her Mama loves her Daddy; our wedding pictures leave no room for doubt that our love is older than, and independent of, her. She knows not only that school is fun and exciting but also that college is where she will go one day. She's seen Daddy's in North Carolina and Mommy's just a city away from home. If it's still around, she will not check the box that says "some high school" for either her mother or father, but her eyes will scan onward and her hand will move down past two-year and four-year and even beyond. And in her four-year-old mind, red, white, and blue automatically means Obama, as in "Look Mommy, she has an Obama bathing suit!"

While phenomenal and amazing, I know that, twenty years from now, it won't matter so much that she's only known a black president her whole young life. Like it did for me, it will matter what she learns from her teachers. What will matter is that she knows she has a teacher-Daddy who reminds her she is loved, she is smart, and she is beautiful. She knows she has a teacher-Mommy who celebrates her rhythm, admires her strength, praises her creativity, and expects her greatness to enhance those around her. What will matter is what all her teachers, coaches, and activity leaders cultivate and inspire in her along the way.

Education at its core is about empowerment. I believe in, and have indeed experienced, its power to unlock doors and break cycles of poverty and incarceration and promote growth and mobility. As teachers, we are integral designers of that empowerment. We have a unique ability to determine what that will look like in our classrooms, with our students. But education's power is diminished, indeed lost, if we leave our young hearts behind.

TWENTY-SEVEN

Look

by Elizabeth Harlan-Ferlo

While teaching about *hijab*, one bra strap slips
off my shoulder, cordons my upper arm.   Some women
in France want to wear it, some in France
want it banned.
I drag a thumb up my arm and yank, hoping not all

the students looking at me
(I'd ordered them moments before: look at me)
will notice, will picture
what I wear under
this wrap-around dress.

* * *

You expect I'll cover this material: rights
of free speech and expression.   Skirts and dresses:
at or below the knee. There's no rule
      saying what I can wear. You expect

I'll be modest. Some women here don't
wear dresses at all.   I cross my ankles. I've learned
by looking—
the custom around here
rather than
what's written down.

* * *

I say: women are free to choose. Some choose   to reclaim

what once was enforced.   I watch the faces
around the squared-off U of tables. I know
what I'm supposed
to get them to see.
I try to feel exactly how close
the layers of my skirt overlap   on my thighs
without looking.

* * *

In a news report I show them
a Frenchman says
      It's uncivilized. Women cannot express themselves.
And it's dangerous. Anyone could hide   under there.
Sometimes when I speak my voice
betrays me. In some places men
cut out their tongues. By now
it's been long enough—
the students sigh, so I tell them: look over
what you've written down. I pause
so as not to slip   and show
something I didn't know
you wanted me
to cover.

TWENTY-EIGHT

Teaching from the Margins

by Monique Cherry-McDaniel

To build community requires vigilant awareness of the work we must continually do to undermine all the socialization that leads us to behave in ways that perpetuate domination.—From bell hooks's *Teaching Community: A Pedagogy of Hope* (2003)

PERIOD TWO

It is 8:35 on a Wednesday morning. My hand is heavy with photocopies, still warm from the copier. It took me an entire planning period to muster the courage to introduce my class of high school seniors to an editorial in a local newspaper. It's titled "Christian Terrorism Is Alive." You see, in a town smack-dab in the middle of the Bible Belt, it is blasphemy to suggest that all terrorists don't have dark hair and brown skin.

I, too mindful of my steps, walk from one aisle to the next and place the appropriate number of articles in the hands of the first student in each row.

"I want you all to take a look at this article; it was printed in last week's newspaper. Jot down what it makes you think about when it comes to religion, terrorism, nationalism, hatred, and media images."

It feels like the class is quieter than usual, but it might just be my paranoid imagination. Only weeks ago I learned from a student why her peers did not seem as excited to read *Kaffir Boy* as they were to read *Catcher in the Rye.*

"It's because you're black, Mrs. Cherry. Nobody wants to say anything that offends you."

"But I'm not South African; I am African American."

"Black is black, Mrs. Cherry. You are just like me."

"In what way?"

"I don't walk around telling people I am Jordanian. To them, A-rab is A-rab."

My mind escapes from the memories of that awkwardly enlightening conversation. Kari asks me to borrow a pen. I give her the one I use to mark the page in the novel we are reading. My eyes don't meet hers; my attention is fixed on Kyle's face. I want to gauge his reaction as he digests the title of the article. But I wander off on another mental journey to three months ago when he wrote in a letter to me that white supremacy isn't an opinion but a fact. I imagine that this article won't sit right with him, and my assumptions are quickly confirmed. After reading the title, he puts the article back on his desk, takes out his cell phone, and begins to send a text message.

Although Kyle disengaged from the article, Christian, a boy who can be characterized only as the epitome of an enigma, has just begun reading it. He tucks his long, dirty-blond locks behind his ears; tips his spectacles over his slender nose; and begins to question. It isn't so much a curious questioning but more like an investigative, incredulous one.

"How do you pronounce the name of this group, Mrs. M. Cherry-McDaniel?" Christian is the only student who insists on referring to me by my entire name.

"It's pronounced 'hoot-a-ree.'"

"Oh. Is it a branch of the Ku Klux Klan?"

"No, Christian. Why would you assume that?"

"Good question, but I think I'll save that material for my written response." He smiles at me, letting me know that he has caught on to my motive for sharing this article with the class.

Ten minutes have passed, and I realize that my breathing and pulse have slowed. I am not as nervous as I was. Soon I hear gasps, whispering, and the students tearing pieces of paper out of notebooks and quickly scribbling their thoughts. I wait as patiently as I can before I solicit responses.

"So, what did you think as you read?"

"Are these Hutaree characters American?" Tyler asks.

"Yes."

"Christians?"

"Yes."

"And—fundamentalists with a wee bit of a violent streak?"

"I would say so."

"Are you collecting this article, 'cause if not, I'm showing this to my dad. This'll teach him that the disciples are kinda gangsta, if you know what I mean."

The class laughs, and my stomach drops. I did not count on anyone wanting to take the article home. In fact, I numbered the corners of each copy to make sure that no student kept a copy.

"The disciples been gangsta. Check your history," says Meriam, a very proud Muslim American student.

"Yeah, but this is undeniable terrorism. Christian terrorism," Dylan retorts. The son of a Baptist pastor, Dylan finds any opportunity to shake organized religion's pedestal.

"Why do we have to call it Christian terrorism? Why isn't it just terrorism?" asks Amy, who has taken it upon herself to be Dylan's most formidable opposition.

"You're right," Dylan exaggerates. "That kinda suggests that all other terrorism is non-Christian terrorism, and that's clearly a falsehood."

Amy smiles, not knowing she has been bested, albeit in the most subtle way.

In order to further the conversation, I pose a question: "How do we label terrorism?" The entire class erupts, *"Muslims!"*

Dave continues the conversation: "I think we *should* call it Christian terrorism. That will force us to accept that what we see on the news isn't the whole story. Like we always say, language is important."

Kyle, not as disengaged as he wants to seem, squares his shoulders so that all the stars and bars on his screen-printed T-shirt will show before he asks, "So what does this article have to do with this book?"

I respond carefully, "Well, Kyle, we're reading a book set in Afghanistan, and I don't want us to judge the characters based on what we think we know about the country or the people."

"Well, can I go to the bathroom?"

"Sure."

The bell rings.

PERIOD SEVEN

I breathe a breath of relief, realizing that I almost have made it through another day, and then I say hello to Emma. She returns my greeting half-heartedly and follows by asking me whether she needs her book today. I give her my "Seriously?!" look, and with just two minutes left before the bell will ring, she turns to rush toward her locker. After I have taken attendance, talked to Megan about what she missed yesterday, and explained to Austin why *irregardless* is not a word, we begin class. We are reading the first scene of *Romeo and Juliet*, and Monica lets me know that she wants to be Benvolio. Brittany quickly claims the part of Mercutio, Chance takes Tybalt, and nobody wants to be George or Sampson, so I decide to read those parts.

The class listens quietly as Sampson threatens to rape or murder the women of the house of Montague. I look up with the hopes of seeing some form of disgust on the students' faces, but I see none. Not one student seems to be taken aback by the blatant and casual violence toward women in the story. I suspect the reactions will be the same when Lord Capulet threatens to beat Juliet for her insolence in refusing to marry Paris. Growing laughter ensues as the banter between the houses of Montague and Capulet continues. However, I cannot laugh. I am still brooding over the previous page. My pulse quickens, and my face flushes as we near the end of the scene. The time has come for me to ask the difficult questions—the questions that have very little do to with the play but everything to do with our world.

"Is anyone a bit put off by the fact that Sampson threatened to rape and kill innocent women?"

The all-too-familiar quiet fills the room, and I am suffocating in my own panic, hoping that one of my students will save me. More quiet.

Austin, with his earbuds securely laced through the gauges in his ears, pipes up with a sure response. "They are at war, right?"

"I struggle with calling it a war, but they are feuding."

"Well, feudin', fightin', fussin'—it's all war. And don't they say all is fair in love and war?"

I expect Austin's response, and I, as usual, carefully consider my answer before I speak. However, Miranda, not so carefully disguising her disdain, responds first.

"Do you see any women participating in the feud-slash-fight-slash-war?"

"Well, no, but they didn't even let girls on the stage back then, remember?" Austin looks to me to confirm his recall of Elizabethan period gender politics, but Miranda is fast in her response.

"It's not about who played the parts; it is about the parts being played. And no, Austin, there are no women fighting with Sampson right now. So, why is it all right for women to be threatened like this?"

Zach speaks up from the back row, "I think we are looking into this a little too seriously. I am sure Shakespeare put this in as comic relief. I mean, who is really taking Sampson seriously?"

Raven and Chance begin to speak at the same time, but Raven yields so Chance can make his comments. "I don't think it's ever funny to threaten rape, whether you are playing or not."

"But this is a book!" Zach retorts in exasperation. "Everybody has read or watched some form of this play, so why are we making a big deal out of it?"

"Rape is a big deal!" Raven finally speaks, and this comment sparks mini conversations all over the room just three minutes before the bell rings. I try to bring some closure to the conversation.

"Zach is right. We have been reading this book for centuries, but I do think we should consider why threatened or real violence against women is considered a casual happening in our society. Let's continue to think about this for tonight."

As all the students file out of the room, some continuing the conversation and others hurrying to make it to their last class, Austin stops me. "Hey, I just want you to know, I really do think rape is bad. It's like a mixture of adultery and stealing, and those are both against the commandments." I nod in acknowledgment of his comment, not quite knowing how to respond.

My day is officially over. For the next hour, as I rearrange desks and chairs, pick up wads of paper, clean the board, bring some semblance of order to my desk, return the dictionaries to the bookshelf, and take final attendance, I will reflect on the fruits and failures of the day. I analyze what my students said and did not say. I count the number of articles I have left from second period. There are nine missing. So, as the last act of the day, I will update my voicemail message to prepare for the parent phone calls I undoubtedly will get by tomorrow morning.

There is no bell to signal that my work is done. My end-of-day ritual has lasted two hours instead of one. I now have a mere hour to have a late lunch and make it to class myself. No happy hour at a swanky bar awaits me, just a group of like-minded individuals who have endured a day not unlike my own. I am eager to get to them; I am eager to see the tired but persistent looks on the faces of my compatriots, those who do the work that cannot be quantified and listed on a state report card. I grab my purse from under my desk, fish for my keys, lock the door behind me, and give thanks for the opportunity to start again tomorrow. I did not disarm a weapon of mass destruction, cure a pandemic, or do anything particularly extraordinary. However, my hope is that the risks I did take in my own warzone of sorts touched somebody who one day would do something extraordinary for humanity.

* * *

These stories are examples of the best and worst of my endeavors to teach social justice in the English classroom. It is not for the faint of heart. It takes hard work, courage, and deliberate and calculated moves to challenge what it means to be a citizen of the world. Teaching social justice in the English classroom requires asking difficult questions of ourselves, of our students, of our curriculum, and of the purpose of schooling as a social necessity.

I believe that any teacher who is committed to teaching the next generation of youth how to be more socially just citizens must understand that living and doing social justice requires vulnerable, dynamic, and organic participation from all parties, that teaching is a political endeavor that requires recognizing and sometimes preferring the counternarrative and the counterpublic. Teaching social justice goes beyond traditional intellectualism and standards-based instruction and enters the realm of organic intellectualism and critical pedagogy, a pedagogy in which the teacher commits to being or living out the struggle of becoming what she or he teaches.

SOCIAL JUSTICE IS PARTICIPATION

Teaching how to live and act in socially just ways requires that we demand of our students a level of presence that is not necessary in our current structures of traditional schooling. Specifically, teaching social justice requires cultivating a space for students, not just to exist but also to exist *consciously*. They must acknowledge their collective and individual interests and the ways they are complicit in their own oppressions and, in some cases, the oppressions of others. This kind of reflective work is exciting, emotional, and political, but it is not easy.

When I started teaching, I knew that teaching social justice would be difficult work, but I never imagined how much trauma and discomfort I would endure daily as a result of demanding that my students and I engage in something more than the traditional ritual of schooling. I had no idea that I would become an expert on reading every roll of the eye, every slouch in a chair, and every long and labored breath as visual and audible reminders of how our curriculum and school culture afford students little opportunity to question, dissent, and grow as citizens of a world much larger than their backyards.

When scholars and practitioners *talk* about teaching social justice in the classroom, we often fantasize about a group of students who are waiting for their civic selves to be awakened. However, when we go about the actual *work* of teaching social justice in the classroom, we encounter a group of students who actually *live* in the world. They watch the news, they publish blogs, they attend political rallies, they work.

The challenge is that students often live in the world uncritically. They "know" who they are, but they do not interrogate how their identities are mediated and influenced by various entities of civil society. They do not realize that very few of their decisions are made independently of normalizing social structures that have existed long before they had a clear gender identity, before they were baptized, before they supported PETA, before they joined "Team Edward," before they "rocked the vote," and before they clicked "Like." In fact, some students identify only in opposition to their peers. Take, for instance, my student Kyle, who assumes his position of white male superiority in opposition to gendered, raced, classed, and otherwise othered students. Take, for instance, my students who understand their religious and political selves only in opposition to negative, often erroneous images of Islam and Muslims.

Any teacher who seeks to prepare socially just citizens must challenge her students' very identities and their most basic assumptions about themselves and their worlds. A teacher of social justice must help students understand, through their own experiences and through the empathetic exploration of their peers' experiences, that positionality matters. Their schools are the perfect places to begin. Have students interrogate the racial disparities of disciplinary records or class enrollment in general and advanced classes. Have students interrogate the classed and gendered disparities in student leadership positions. Have them explore and articulate the problem of a female-dominated teaching force being governed by a male-dominated school administrative team. Help them recognize how similar sorts of disparities exist in other spheres of our local, national, and global society, and then help them to recognize how these disparities perpetuate social injustice on a global scale. The possibilities for this kind of academic and civic engagement are endless if only we would change our paradigm about the purpose of schooling and the outcomes we seek.

* * *

As I end this piece, I imagine the click-clack of my smart and comfortable teacher pumps hitting the shiny linoleum floors of my school building. My gait is slow, my breathing is easy, and my spirit is right. I walk toward the silhouette of a student. It is Kyle, sitting on the floor, propped up against a bank of lockers. He is engrossed in a book. As I approach him, I see that it is a copy of Khaled Hosseini's *The Kite Runner*. He looks up from the book, haphazardly folds the top corner of the page, closes the book, and quickly shoves it into his tattered book bag. There is something sticking out of the bag; I recognize it as one of the nine missing copies of the article we read in class today. I smile at him. He may not know it yet, but I do. He is changing, and it is for the better.

"Have a good night, Kyle."

"You too, Mrs. Cherry."

"As it turns out, I will."

Hmm, yes. I will, indeed.

TWENTY-NINE

Peace

by Walter Enloe

I. OASIS OF PEACE

This village sits like a diamond in the sun
From there is seen the entire world,
Calling God's name to draw her near,
Birds of peace circling from above,
Crying from the eagle, cooing from the dove.
And then it lands and settles down at our school—
An Oasis of Peace—
That same oasis I find in my heart wherever I am.
Peace does begin with me,
And others have found it in the now silence of Auschwitz
And Anne Frank's home,
In the internment and concentration camps of American
Citizens in my hometown,
At the Cenotaph among all the doves of Hiroshima Peace Park,
And then by the river we found it within and between
Ourselves—
An Oasis of Peace.
When doves were crying
Martin Luther King told us the simplest truth:
"The world is more and more a neighborhood.
But is it any more of a human-hood?
If we don't learn to live together as brothers and sisters
We shall perish together as fools."

Take these small paper birds of peace, folded with our hands
For the world to know
That children want peace—
They teach us that learning to fold a paper bird,
A crane or dove,
Is like becoming a peacemaker.
You make mistakes
You start over.
You learn from others.
You don't do it alone.
So with our Oasis of Peace,
Built and nurtured out of evil and ashes.
And so the doves cried
Oasis of Peace.

II. OASIS OF PEACE

In this place called Hiroshima,
There is an island where all kids may feel safe
And inspired to help the world.
It is a place where you will sit down next to her,
Next to the human being who is laughed at
And called names just because she talks different, looks
Different,
Walks different, thinks different
Acts different.
You will sit down next to her and befriend her,
Because when you get to know each other
You will find out you are pretty much the same
About a lot of things.
You feel and you laugh
And you cry like cranes and doves.
You have dreams and you have hopes,
For you want to be a friend
And you want to have a friend.
For all of you know
What it is like to be treated differently
Because you are labeled a color
Or gender, nation or an "other"
While riding the same little blue marble of a planet
Spinning and spinning, around and around
In search of places that are oases,

Places where doves coo in the hands of children.
Shalom. Heiwa. Oasis of Peace

THIRTY

You Gotta Be Ready for Some Serious Truth to Be Spoken

by Debra Busman

To teach "Creative Writing and Social Action," you gotta be ready for some serious truth to be spoken. When you ask students to break silence, to bear witness, to connect the meaning of their own personal lives to the larger societal frame, you gotta be ready for the truths that fly out, crawl out, peep out, and scream out from underneath the thick walls of practiced silence. You gotta be ready for stories of border crossings, coyotes and cops, night beatings, gunshots and chemo, pesticides, HIV, AZT, protease inhibitors, and the pink-cheeked nineteen-year-old who says, "Hey, next Tuesday I'll have *five years* clean and sober; can we have a cake in class?" You gotta be ready for stories that start, *"Ese pinche* Columbus didn't have no stinkin' green card." You gotta be ready for the straight-A student who has to leave school because her INS paperwork hasn't come through, and the social security number she gave at registration was the first nine numbers that came to her mind, and she cannot get financial aid because she is "illegal."

To teach "Creative Writing and Social Action," you gotta be ready for all the stories, whether you want to hear them or not. When you ask students to speak the truths of their lives, you gotta be ready for the Stanford-bound future teacher of America who writes about being kicked out of the Navy for being too racist. You gotta be ready for the sweet-faced, curly-haired lover of Jesus who writes stories of his days as a violent skinhead, beating up blacks, Jews, and queers. You gotta be ready for the stories the young man cannot yet share in class, scribbles slid under your office door, 4:30 a.m. e-mails, telling of his father's rage, the belt, the whiskey, the steel pipe slammed down hard on the thin nine-year-old boy body. The father's last words, before he left the child cowering in the corner, his back broken in two places: "Be a man, you pussy. I better not see you cry."

To teach "Creative Writing and Social Action," you gotta be ready for war stories unlike those CNN sound bites about "precision bombs" and "surgical air strikes" spoon-fed into the comfort of our living-room TV sets during Desert Storm. You gotta be ready for the glassy-eyed reefer-smoking closeted ex-GI to suddenly bust out with long-held stories of "friendly fire" and "collateral damage," stories told through choked sobs about retrieving the remains of his eight buddies, all under twenty years old, from their burned-out carcass of a tank, bombed the night before by an "American mistake." You gotta be ready when he tells the class, "Man, you guys gotta know, war is not the fuckin' video game you think it is," when he tells stories of standing guard duty with no ammunition, stories of surrendering Iraqi soldiers shot en masse, thumbs and ears cut off for souvenirs, bodies bulldozed into shallow sand graves.

To teach "Creative Writing and Social Action," you gotta be ready for these stories to share space with the one by the retired prison guard, now a minister and college student, who writes of his experience as a young African American police officer on the scene with five white sheriffs in 1960s rural Mississippi when a seventeen-year-old gas station robbery suspect, a young black man whose family he knew, was thrown into the back of a squad car, handcuffed, and locked inside with a 120-pound German Shepherd police dog that was ordered to attack. Then, when the writer describes the ensuing screams, the beer bellies, spit, and cigars, the white laughter, the blood, the horrific carnage told forty years later with such immediacy and precision, you can only hold your heart and say, "Oh, good lord, why did I ever stress the importance of using sensory details, concrete language, and vivid imagery?"

To teach "Creative Writing and Social Action," you gotta be ready to hear the stories held in private silence the past four years by a young woman working with the local Rape Crisis Center, stories about rape, domestic violence, child sexual abuse—things she says she didn't think you were "supposed to talk about in college," at least not until she took a women's studies class and "Intro to Creative Writing." It means you gotta be ready for the young Japanese American student who drifts through class, quiet and respectful, suddenly shocked into consciousness by the poetry of Janice Mirikitani, suddenly alive and angry and writing poem after poem after poem about Executive Order 9066, model minorities, identity, resistance, and rice, practically busting down your office door one day in his excitement to tell you he finally realized what he would write his senior capstone paper on. "The camps," he says. "I'm going to write about the camps. Both my grandmothers were sent to the internment camps. I'm going to interview them over break, get their stories, get the truth of my history." Then, you gotta be ready when he slumps into your office following spring break, crestfallen. "They wouldn't talk about it," he says. "They told me everything else, all about their lives before the war, how they decorated their houses, how they fell in love with their husbands; they told me all about my parents when they were babies, about their family businesses. But they wouldn't talk about the camps. They just shut up, looked at me funny, said, 'There is nothing to say.' It's weird; it scared me. Like whenever I brought it up, they just turned into some other people, like they weren't my grandmas any more. They are eighty years old. I don't want to hurt them, so I had to stop asking. What am I going to do? My project is ruined. I have no stories." And you have to tell him, "No, your project is not ruined. There are worlds within those silences. Your story is just beginning."

To teach "Creative Writing and Social Action," you gotta be ready for the young blond girl from a private high school in Sacramento's suburbs who rolls her Maybelline eyes the first day of class and says, "Is this going to be one of those courses where they try and ram that multicultural crap down your throat?" The same girl who weeks later sits weeping in class, heart and mind open, listening to shared stories of INS thugs and deported grandfathers and pesticide-poisoned baby brothers, wheezing from asthma. Stories about cousins orphaned by police bombs dropped on fellow family MOVE members, seven- and nine-year-old brother and sister taken from their home, sitting in the Philadelphia police station, surrounded by cops watching the bombing live and in color on TV news, laughing, telling the children, "See those flames. See those tanks. That's your daddy inside there. That's your daddy we finally got right where he belongs." And the young, blond, private-high-school student, who truly believed that California always belonged to the United States and that racism ended with the abolition of slavery, or at the very least after Martin Luther King Jr.'s "I Have a Dream" speech, turns her face to the class, Maybelline running down her cheeks, and says, "I'm so sorry. I didn't know. They never taught me about any of this. I'm so sorry. I just never knew." And her workshop buddy, Aisha, the self-described Pan-Africanist revolutionary, takes the girl in her arms, rocks her softly. And Carlos, sitting in the back, can't help but shake his head, muttering, "Damn. And they got the nerve to tell me that *my people* are underprepared for college."

To teach "Creative Writing and Social Action," you gotta be ready for the student who, having just listened to your best rap on the wonders of metaphoric imagery, says, "You know, Professor Busman, I mean, I don't mean no disrespect or nothing, but, you know, all that stuff you been saying about metaphors and similes and shit, I mean, it's cool and everything, and I can see it working good in some poems, but my poem, you know, when I talk about that cop smashing the side of Bobby's skull with his stick, well, I don't want people to think that that noise sounds like anything other than the sound of a motherfuckin' pig's billy club crackin' up against the side of a brother's head. I mean *that's* the sound. It don't sound like nothing else. I don't want people *thinking* it sounds like something else. And, that line where I put my fist into that concrete wall out behind County General, I don't want people thinking that that feels like anything other than a fist into a concrete wall. Sometimes things ain't 'like' anything else; they just are what they are, and the reader just gonna have to deal with it. You know what I'm saying?"

To teach "Creative Writing and Social Action," you gotta be ready to learn at least fifteen times more than whatever it is you think you have to teach. It means you gotta be ready to accept the fact that you can never really be ready for all the confusion, the grief, and the wonder that enters the classroom when students take you at your word and believe you really do want to hear the full and messy truths of all their "wild and precious" lives.

THIRTY-ONE

Reflection Questions for Part Four: Teaching against the Grain

1. In this section, writers describe their efforts to teach against the standardized grain. What are some of the ways the writers do so, both pedagogically and curricularly?

2. What are some of the strategies Monique Cherry-McDaniel describes in her narrative, "Teaching from the Margins," to engage her students in critical thinking related to social justice issues? How might you adapt her strategies for your own classroom or context?

3. In his poem "Peace," Walter Enloe writes, "Peace does begins with me." What does that mean for us as educators? How might we prepare ourselves to be bearers of peace, to make our classrooms oases, especially for students who feel marginalized at school?

Part Five

Speaking Up and Talking Back

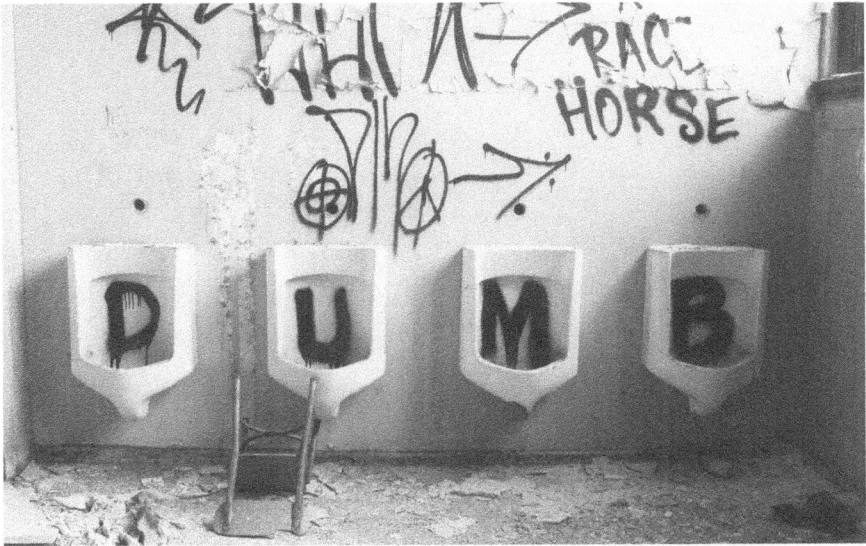

THIRTY-TWO

Through My Eyes

by Cinthia Suasti

Through my eyes, the color of my skin decides
how much freedom and privilege i deserve.
But I believe it should be based on how much i've worked.

Through my eyes, to attend college I must change
the pronunciation of my name, my clothes. I must adopt a new identity:
an identity that I have seen slowly fade
like my people's history in school textbooks.

Through my eyes, obtaining a high school diploma
should not feel like a privilege when it is a right.
As students, our right to an education was taken away
the moment our teachers were convinced
that we'll just go flip burgers at mcdonalds
or clean bathrooms
for the rest of our lives.

I want to break these chains of oppression
to prove que si se puede a mi gente.
Little do these teachers know that we'll be the next lawyers,
doctors, and scientists.
Unfortunately, this will not happen unless we break these chains
because this educational system was never meant to teach people
como yo.
Whatever that means. I am just like everyone else.

For as long as I can remember, we've been told

to follow the rules and not question anything.
But why is that?
Is it because we're meant to surrender to authority
or because we're still seen as the minority,
even though we're the new majority?
It is time to accept that people's intellect
is based on determination and dedication,
not race or discrimination,

and we all deserve an equal education.

THIRTY-THREE

Playground Futurities

by James F. Woglom and Stephanie Jones

The country's commitment to socialism and class struggle, however, wasn't completely eliminated during Mussolini's rule and something extraordinary emerged from the ashes of oppression and violence.

An abandoned German tank was sold by locals in a village outside Reggio Emilia to build a school for workers' children. Working-class and poor folks had suffered the most under Mussolini's regime and in his war, and something had to be done immediately to begin righting the wrongs.

Loris Malaguzzi heard about the building of this new school and joined in the effort where resistance against Fascism was laid with each brick leftover from bombed homes in the village.

Once the school was opened, Malaguzzi used pedagogies in distinct contrast to obedience and suppression. Creativity, innovation, critical thinking, and class equity were emphasized and across decades, Reggio Emilia systematically constructed early childhood education centers to support the working-classes, build cross-class alliances, and encourage a strong sense of self, community, and autonomy in young children.

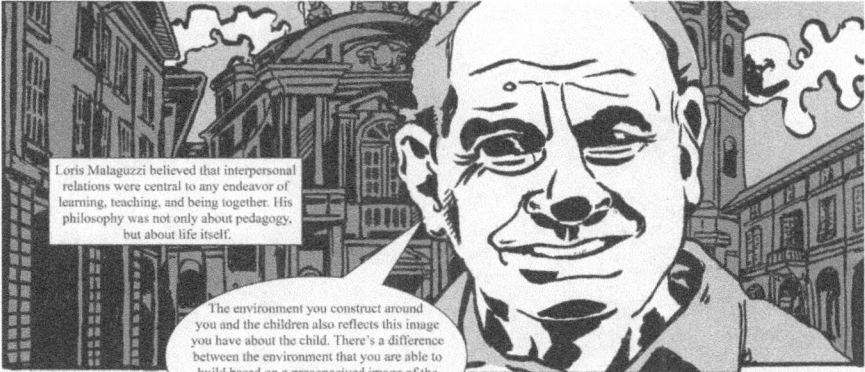

Loris Malaguzzi believed that interpersonal relations were central to any endeavor of learning, teaching, and being together. His philosophy was not only about pedagogy, but about life itself.

The environment you construct around you and the children also reflects this image you have about the child. There's a difference between the environment that you are able to build based on a preconceived image of the child and the environment that you can build that is based on the child you see in front of you.

Many U.S. educators have been drawn to the child-centered practices, but, the irony that primarily economically advantaged children benefit from these pedagogies in mostly private school settings in the U.S. is not yet a broadly discussed concern.

Loris Malaguzzi International Centre "A dedicated meeting place where professional development and research intersect for people in Reggio Emilia, Italy and the world who wish to innovate education and culture."

It is our assertion that all children are subjects with rights who should be provided rich, dynamic, intentionally-designed environments where they are free to explore, create, and problem-solve with minimal adult intervention, regardless of their means.

It is a crucial irony to consider, though, because underlying Reggio's insistence that children are subjects with rights, is a long history of class struggle, socialism, and a country's fight against Fascism, and in only offering differing views of the world to a privileged few, we limit the continuation of that history.

The grown-ups are often the ones who struggle at the Clubhouse. They have to re-learn how to be in the world outside the micro-fascisms imposed on themselves and others. Grown-ups tend to see structures built for them by other people, like a simple slide, as having one required use.

Even very young children, however, become bored with the predictable outcome of sitting on one's bottom and sliding through a tube.

Those moments of unpredictability, of creative improvisation that makes something new out of the old, make a lot of grown-ups anxious as they struggle with not already knowing the outcome.

If those folks in that village near Reggio Emilia so long ago could only perceive one use for a tank, people in every part of the world wouldn't be talking about their approach to early childhood education as everyday utopias. These utopias are dynamic spaces committed to relational ways of being, spaces that are never done, never finalized, always in process and becoming.

At least once a month at the Clubhouse, an idea takes hold and spreads through the modestly sized building. One by one children and grown-ups will set aside their individual pursuits and join a thread that stitches them together in being differently, living a utopia today – a playground futurity fueled by an aesthetic way of being in the world that is, we argue, a preferable way of living.

Staged rituals and ceremonies, theater, jewelry stores, fashion shows, dance parties, concerts, painting over unwelcome language on picnic tables, and full service restaurants have all manifested in these joint performances of 25+ young people aged between 5 and 14, with the teacher education students right by their sides.

Recruitment, preparation, negotiation, orchestration, and the making of costumes, props, choreography, lines, songs, music, and so on culminate in the production of something that only became possible because we were all - children and teacher education students and teacher educator - willing to lean into unpredictability and imagine something new in our togetherness.

Micro-utopias are not without conflict, turmoil, and even sadness, but they are a possible space in which we may live in resistance to micro-fascisms. Relational aesthetics can give our U.S. education a real purpose today, a purpose that speaks to humanity and our relationships with ourselves and the world. The work of educators, including teacher educators, then, might be to design spaces and relations where such micro-utopias have the possibility of emerging.

THIRTY-FOUR

The Richest Country in the World: A Fable

by LouAnn Johnson

"If you don't learn to read, you can't go to college," warned the clever people. "We don't care," said the little numbers. "We care!" boomed the colleges. "We need students." So the suits told the teachers to give the students passing grades.

"But children should not go to college if they cannot read!" cried the teachers. "It is your fault that the children cannot read," answered the clever people.

Many little numbers refused to accept the easy grades. Some of them sneaked out of school in broad daylight. The suits hired people to hunt down the truants.

They locked up the worst little numbers and threw away the key. "That will teach them," said the suits. But it did not teach them and it was not good.

Then, one day a very important report was published.

> **Very Important Report**
>
> Who **can** read:
> - most Europeans
> - everybody in Costa Rica
> - most Australians
> - Africans who go to school
>
> Who **cannot** read:
> - people in poverty-stricken third-world countries
> - Many children in the richest country in the world

The clever people were appalled and enraged. "We have the wealthiest athletes and the most TV talk shows!" they cried. "How can they say our children cannot read? We'll show them." And they built even bigger schools.

They hired so many adults that they broke the school budgets. "We need help," the clever people told the government.

"Oh no! We have no money for schools," said the powerful people (whose own children attended private schools). "You must help yourselves."

So, the clever people closed many schools. They cut fine arts programs. They opened their doors to the soda and candy vendors who paid millions to put their irresistible shiny machines in the schools.

The children grew fatter every year, and many of them developed diabetes.

With no elbowroom, and no music or art to brighten the long days, the poorly nourished little numbers became even more disruptive. Some became cruel and tormented others.

But the schools were so huge that the suits couldn't catch the bullies. They didn't know the bullies' names.

© 2002 LouAnne Johnson

3

The numbers continued to complain and misbehave and try to escape from their educational prisons. And like their adult counterparts, some planned violent takeovers.

Huge Public School

They brought weapons into the schools and blasted their anger into the walls and the chalkboards and their fellow numbers.

"What is wrong with these children?" cried the clever people.

"It's television!" shouted some people.

"It's sex education," suggested some poorly educated people.

We must do something!

The business community offered to help. But, alas! Some of them had lost sight of their mission...

"We can make people feel good about having something wrong with them," said the money-hungry sector of professional people helpers.

"And we can make them buy whatever we tell them they need," said the advertisers.

Rx   U R Nuts   Buy this!

"People love prescription medications," said the pharmaceutical companies.

This psychological-pharmaceutical-advertising conglomerate came up with a most clever idea ...

There was something wrong with THE CHILDREN'S BRAINS...

Brain Farts?

The clever conglomerate designed special tests and drugs and advertisements. They created a psychological condition and diagnosed the little numbers who hated school.

They prescribed drugs to calm down the little numbers and make them sit in their chairs and stop trying to escape.

The clever conglomerate told the parents that they weren't to blame for their children's behavior and the parents were so grateful. And indeed many little numbers became very docile.

OK. OK. OK.

But other little numbers refused to believe that their brains were broken.

"We are not numbers!" cried the children in despair. "If you treated us like human beings, we would show you how smart we can be."

challenge me and I'll work   Be Kind to Kids   Say No to drugs!

More and more numbers refused to learn to read. "They can learn," insisted the clever people. "They are just stubborn - but we can make them learn."

© 2002 LouAnne Johnson

"We will give them terribly hard tests," said the clever people. "If they do not pass, they can stay in the same grade until they rot." They told the teachers to teach the tests.

"We do not want to teach children to take tests," cried the teachers. "We must teach them to read and write and think and create."

"Piffle!" said the clever people. "If students fail the tests, we'll test you and prove that you are the reason they cannot read." "Let us use our brains," the students cried, but the clever people ignored them.

And some compassionate adults listened. They created personal programs for students.

The compassionate adults welcomed all students to their programs—rich and poor, gifted and troubled, chocolate and vanilla and peach and caramel.

They spent the budgets on children, not adults. They called the children by name. The children behaved and learned their lessons and it was very, very good.

Soon, there were dozens, then hundreds of small personal programs. The small programs blossomed and thrived—and the clever conglomerate became jealous.

We're in big trouble!

"We look bad," they whispered among themselves. "Whatever shall we do?"

"We could try to be more like the small personal schools," suggested a clever person. "What a brilliant idea!" cried the others. They held many important meetings.

They discussed and debated and designed and designated. They reorganized and researched and rescheduled and revised. They coordinated and delegated and overhauled and updated.

And, finally, in the richest country in the world ...

The children began to learn to read

The Beginning

©2002 LuAnne Johnson

THIRTY-FIVE

Three Spaces of Exclusion: The 21st-Century High School Integration of That Girl

by V. Thandi Sulé

I am that girl
Black, fat, and dark *skin-ded*
I can fill the universe with my imagination
But in this space
In this hallway
I am translucent
Enveloped by Miriams, Amys, and Abigails
We rub shoulders
We touch
We smile
But they don't really want to know me
Because I am that girl
Black, fat, and dark *skin-ded*
Just one generation away from Kool-Aid and government cheese
So my words don't always sound proper
My tongue dances with letters, dropping those that mess up my rhythm
Laughter
Dumb
Did I say something dumb?
I wonder as they, those Miriams, Amys, and Abigails
Insist on correcting me
So I stuff myself inside myself

Strap on my Ruby Bridges and glide down the hallway
like a Mofo in a Spike Lee dolly shot
But I'm feigning confidence
While my insides rot.

Dat girl is me
I sit in the first row,
Trying not to turn around
'Cause I already know.
Everybody's gonna know my name
Because my singularity, my epidermis *is* the diversity
I'm that shy, smart, kinky-haired Black girl
Nobody acknowledges
But everybody knows
I know my difference is not a curiosity
Just an exception
I swallow all of the stereotypes
Let them marinate in my DNA
I puke anxiety
I ask too many questions

Did that Geophysics teacher just say I might be more comfortable
    in Earth Science?
I defecate self-doubt
But with Little Rock Nine buried in my armpit
I don't sleep
Imhotep burrows in my brain
Make no mistake
I speak to the Earth, I become its student and its teacher.
Failure is not an option.
Average is not an option
When I leave this class
They will remember me
Even if they do not know me.

Who's that?
Tar baby
I hear.

Precious
I hear, laughter.

Nobody
I hear, silence.

The cafeteria serves both belongingness and exclusion.

No one awaits me.
I am disposable.
I try to laugh at the right times but I don't understand their jokes
Or am I the joke?
I suffocate in angst
If loneliness had a companion, it would be me.
At lunchtime, the stairway becomes my sanctuary
The shoe prints—temporary companions
But their impermanence reminds me that this ghetto of solitude is deafening
Discovering my tongue, I scream
Discovering my voice, I die
Hemorrhaging life
I escape.

Music is my salve
With each song I create a reality where . . .

I am that girl
Black, fat and dark *skin-ded*
Unleashed by colorblind liberalism
Unhinged by never-mind multiculturalism
Unfettered by undermined egalitarianism

Unmasked.

THIRTY-SIX
They Said

by Sarah Gilbertson

I see you they said
You with your Red braid,
Your glasses, your crooked teeth.
I know you they said.
You with your homeschooled education and quiet demeanor.
I recognize you they said
You with your freckles
Shy smile and eyes at the ground.

You are
Clumsy.
They said.
You are
Awkward.
They said.
You are
A follower.

They said.

I see me I said.
I am a unique
and complex Individual.
I know me I said.
I am passionate about life,
About art, about humanity.

I recognize me I said.
As a girl that
Will make a difference one day.

I am
Confident
I said.
I am
Creative.
I said.
I am
A leader.

I said.

We see them they said.
Those kids with their baggy clothes
And braided locks.
We know them they said.
Those kids with their slang language
And bad manners.
We recognize them they said.
As kids with gangs,
and guns and ill-intentions.

Those kids are
trouble.
They said
Those kids are
Dangerous.
They said.
Those kids are
Doomed.

They said.

We see YOU, we said.
You and your ignorant ways.
We know YOU, we said.
You and your narrow thoughts.
We recognize YOU, we said.
As someone with little faith in us.

You are
Misguided.
We said.

You are
Confused.
We said.
You are
Wrong.

We say.

We are worthy.

THIRTY-SEVEN

Language as Weapon: Lessons from the Front Lines

by Lani T. Montreal

How much we don't see when we look only for deficiency, when we tally up all that people can't do. —Mike Rose, "Crossing Boundaries," *Lives on the Boundary*

As a composition instructor, grading student work is the part of my job I most dislike. Letting my students know that I had caught another sentence boundary or syntax error is no fun. Sometimes I have students read their writing out loud to me, hoping that they will discover their mistakes themselves. Most of them do, but some read aloud and then look at me and ask, "So? Where's my mistake?" Indeed. What they have read is coherent and conveys their meaning well. Now, am I implying that their English is wrong? Am I saying that the English they have learned from their elders and their elders' elders is wrong? Who am I to say that they are wrong? Born outside of the United States, I am not American, nor do I speak American. What makes my Filipino-accented English more acceptable?

"Well, I am not saying that what you just read is wrong, but you do have some grammar errors." And here, I launch into my usual speech about the academic world being their gateway to success in the real world but that, before they can even get into this world, they have to learn its language well. "It's just like joining a club. If you can't communicate the way everybody in the club does, then you can't be part of it."

After reading Noah Eli Gordon's essay "From Error to Error: On Dysgraphia," I doubt not just the wisdom of this advice, but also its pedagogical implications. Gordon shares his experience grappling with a learning disability that is defined as, and he quotes the Oxford English Dictionary, an "inability to write coherently." As a narrative, he paints a vivid picture of tortuous attempts at normalcy; as a rhetorical essay, Gordon compellingly argues against the oppressive formalism that underscores the rationale for freshman writing programs.

Gordon's essay also reminds me of my own "tangled" relationship with English, which I now embrace like a close friend with whom I once had a falling out but now have forgiven. Growing up under the Marcos regime in the Philippines, I associated English with a fearsome man on the television telling me not to litter or loiter after dark.

I no longer remember from where I got the notion—the drunken debates among my parents' friends at parties; dinner-table diatribes; my uncle disappearing for three days and coming home battered, bruised, and riddled with mosquito bites after he was "picked up" by Ferdinand Marcos's blue-uniformed Metrocom, enforcers of the midnight curfew, and taken to Camp Crame, the military prison, my mother frantic, pulling every discernible string to find him, begging for someone to set him free, but I knew even as a little girl that this martial law was wrong and that the moon-faced president who interrupted Saturday afternoon cartoons with his impeccable English was not to be trusted—not his edicts, not his songs, not his books. And so I hated studying history and its coherent lies in English. Instead, I favored the incoherent conversation in Tagalog overheard at the corner store, the gossip in school about the rebel nun who took to the mountains to teach literacy to indigenous children, the washed-out writing on the walls calling Marcos "Tuta ng U.S. Imperialismo," the stooge of U.S. imperialism. *"Im-pe-ri-al-is-mo. Ano yan, dad?"* I asked as the Jeepney rode past the graffiti. "It's best that you do not know, honey."

Nevertheless, I tried to get to know it well, this language of power and glamor, tried to understand the mystique, the hullabaloo over my classmate Gina's composition about her "fabulous" summer in Disneyland, Cory's "wonderful" trip to a five-star beach resort in a country where over half the population did not even have clean water.

Here now in the United States, in the belly of the beast that coddled the dictator in his last days, I have brandished my English to get across borders, lay claim to a coveted position, and take my rightful place at the Ikea checkout counter. I would like to think it has also provided me with a VIP pass to Club Academia. Despite all this, though, my English still feels short. I never could quite understand those damn idioms, not to mention those pesky prepositions. (Imagine the combination! "We are all on/in the same boat?") Certainly, my professors in graduate school, with their kind commentary in the margins and less subtle reminders for correct grammar usage, did much to coax coherence into my insecure English.

I remember Erwin, whose first attempt at one of my unimaginative prompts as a starting comp instructor yielded a burst of unbridled creative writing: "I felt like a character in a play; they wanted me to perform—sing and dance in a stylized manner for their amusement. It was not a part I auditioned for; nor was it a part I wanted to play. I refused to paint my face white, buck my eyes, extend my lips or lower my intellectual parlance." Erwin, a black, middle-aged photographer returning to school after many years, could not spell without the spell-checker or punctuate properly. He refused to fit into any subcategory that came from a developmental learning study that was done to support or debunk the idea of remediation. I appealed the failed results of his ENGLISH 100 exit essay that semester, and now, years later, I continue to help him edit his submissions to literary journals.

Ah, my basic writing students and their vain attempts at the coherence being imposed upon them: They come brimming with stories and ideas that cannot be contained neatly on the white page, and we do not think twice about slashing words and inserting arrowheads between phrases to indicate a missing word or punctuation. Unleash the wrath of Grammatika upon them whose Englishes are deemed unacceptable by the academy—grammatically incorrect, abysmal, incoherent.

In his essay, Gordon shared how he was institutionalized many times for failing to conform—not just academically but also behaviorally. "Education took a backseat to simple containment," he explained. Often I wonder if our draconian attitude toward error in student writing might be stifling creative and critical thinking in the same way. Gordon, now a published author and English professor, gave an unsettling account of the experience of students deemed remedial or labeled with learning disability in the past, but what have we learned since then? Have we become more compassionate in these times, more reflective about the ways in which we negotiate power and privilege in our classrooms?

I remember having a conversation with peers who genuinely cared about their students but insisted that, really, it's not about race or class; it's just about writing coherently. "It is the writing we are assessing, not the writer," they claimed, when we require them to compose a coherent essay in an hour and a half, something many of us struggle to do. (I know because it took me weeks to declare this piece of writing worthy of submission.) But what of another instructor's experience who, after exhausting every possible active, as well as computer-assisted, instructional strategy, gets a lesson from her own student about how he learned to write better? This student, she said, had been failing the class but wrote an impressive in-class essay one day. She took him aside and asked how he finally "got it."

"I just took my cousin's advice," he said. "He told me to write 'white.'"

THIRTY-EIGHT

Starfish (A Practical Exorcism)

by Kyle "Guante" Tran Myhre

I am standing in a school or a submarine. Everything is gray and the walls
can almost kiss each other. Children avalanche around my legs. It is too dark
here. And my job these days is to turn all the lights on and pretend to be brave.

We smell like unused paintbrushes; the air is still, hanging just over this river
or this sewer pipe full of hands and shoes and teeth. I see a teacher in a window,
a smiley face painted onto a crash-test dummy. I forget where I am going.

These children will grow up to be scarecrows. These children will snarl once
at the world and they will be put down. These children will grow into the poems
written about them, live in the spaces between the letters and shiver

when the books open. And my job these days is to melt the winter with a flashlight.
I work in after-school program purgatory, moving from school to school siphoning
tears and collecting poems. I keep the poems in a shiny leather briefcase;

I dump the tears out in the parking lot. And my job these days is to identify bodies.
My job these days is to be the Disney World full-body suit Sisyphus. My job
these days is to dream of starfish, tens of thousands smothered by the air on the beach

being pulled apart alive by the seagulls. I toss a few back into the ocean and people
tell me that I'm making a difference. But there is no honor in triage, only necessity.
And these children: they need something more than another plucky white woman

to pry them open and extract their genius, or one more straight-A Teach for
America mirage trying to "save" them, or one more positive male role model
teaching them how to write poetry. And my job these days is to be one more

positive male role model teaching them how to write poetry, and it's killing me.
A teacher once told me that this is the curse of direct service—we make a difference,
just not enough of one. We are the bricks in a haunted house, doing an admirable

job keeping the ceiling from collapsing but not able to remove the evil from the air.
And my job these days is to be a hack exorcist. My job these days is to be
a superhero in a coma, a strip-mall Santa Claus. My job these days is to blindly

feel my way through the jagged corners of these schools and not bleed too much.
And suddenly I remember where I'm going: the guidance counselor,

who is concerned that one of my students might be unstable because she

wrote a poem about death, not knowing that death and suffering are pretty
much all 15-year-olds write about. On my way to the office, an impossibly small boy
from one of my sessions cannonballs through the crowd, punches me in the shoulder

and says, "thank you." His name is Brian. He says thank you and means it. And I'm
stuck, somewhere between "you're welcome" and "I'm sorry." I'm stuck staring
at banners: attitude is everything, no child left behind, I love my school. I'm stuck.

And my job these days is not to make a difference, it is to fight, with everything
I have, for a world in which I don't have to. My job these days is to try
and find a way to be both brick and builder, to teach starfish to fly.

THIRTY-NINE
All the Ways We Learn

by Sarita Gonzales

my father
battle scars decades long
stretch across his brown skin
I remember
he used to always grab me by my arm and
whisper: mija, education.

at 15
he was king of the barrio
in San Antonio
ruling the streets
with fists and fear (hand like loaded gun)
50 years later
they still bow to him
when we go there
he points out dilapidated buildings
bustling avenidas
and unchanged bus lines that mark his memories
like he marked those territories.

stories told like lectures to me
growing up
but in college
I schooled the poli sci professor
on the politics of a cease fire
see even the streets whisper,

education.

his silver streaked mustache twitches now
as he recalls the poverty
steel green government trucks
kicking up dust
as they delivered
monthly commodities

brown eyed children
would pause in their play
watch their mamas curse.

right on time the pig farmers would cruise on through
scoop up these welfare "freebies"
everybody knew
only their pigs could put them to any good use
children suddenly feel too old for games
and discrimination whispers,
education.

my father's got 65 years of stories just like those
resting on these narrow shoulders
I'm here to tell you
there is a hefty price to pay for all that learning
he still wields a gun
his mouth shoots words
like bullets
I can't seem to dodge.

I'm holding on to this idea
our futures
are not sealed like our histories
I'm walking through doors he kicked down for me
with my brown skin
I have climbed to the top of these very ivory towers
I still believe
knowledge is power,

so I'll take it
his life
my experiences
your dreams
our aspirations
so we may understand
that all of it

all of this . . .
whispers
education.

FORTY

we pull the wool over this rainbow of eyes: the archeology of white people (pts. 1 and 2)

by Paul Thomas

I was a white girl in a crowd of white girls in the park—"Pink Rabbits,"
The National

"They're such beautiful shirts," she sobbed, her voice muffled in the
thick folds. "It makes me sad because I've never seen such—such beautiful shirts before." —Daisy, *The Great Gatsby*, F. Scott Fitzgerald

THE ARCHEOLOGY OF WHITE PEOPLE (PT. 1)

> we gather into schools all our children
> red brown yellow black and white
> leaving them all blue
>
> we continue to serve them
> Fitzgerald and Hemingway
> the archeology of white people
>
> a Lost Generation fabricated to fool
> cigarettes chandeliers and swimming pools
> such glorious decadent people
>
> all lined up in rows of pastel shirts
> like Jordan almonds or Easter eggs

"In his blue gardens men and girls
came and went like moths
among the whispering
and the champagne and the stars."

Ignore the body in the road
we whisper in their tiny innocent ears
Isn't that golden car spectacular?

THE KINDNESS SCHOOL
(BEYOND THE ARCHEOLOGY OF WHITE PEOPLE, PT. 2)

it simply happened one day
when the teachers decided
enough was enough

all the boys with OCD
spent the day playing drums
or riding their bicycles

and the introverts sat quietly
smiling periodically in the corners
while the extroverts laughed and laughed

and soon the pleasures became many
as varied as the children themselves
until one day a child stood to proclaim

after reading *Hamlet* all on her own
"I say, we will have no more tests"
to which there was thunderous cheering

yes it seemed simple and obvious enough
the founding of the kindness school
with open doors and children singing

FORTY-ONE

Use your words!

by Mary Elizabeth Hayes

Jugando
Bailando
Imaginando
    Use your words.
Sigo con mi juego.
Con mi amiga.
    Me pasas los colores?
    Ten.
        Use your words, girls.
Sonreímos y nos miramos—
brillantes los ojitos.
    Yo soy la mamá, y ésa es mi bebé, Isabela.
    Yo puedo ser el papá. Soy bombero.
        Guys! Use your words.
Mejor no hablo.
Un libro con rostro blanco y cabello dorado.
    Maestra, no entiendo.
    Me ayudas a leerlo?
        Use your words, please.
Entonces qué?
Cómo las uso?
Acaso no son *mis* palabras las que están saliendo de *mi* boca?
De mi ser?
De mi corta historia?
Son los sonidos que conozco desde que nací.

Son las palabras de mi mamá.
De mi papá.
De mis hermanos y mis abuelos que viven en Skype.
Me han servido de mucho.
Para todo.
Hasta hoy.
Hasta que *tú* llegaste en *mi* vida.
Acaso no son palabras?
Y cuándo yo aprenda, te miraré
y te diré
> *Use* my *words.*

Translation

Playing
Dancing
Make believe
> *Use your words.*

I keep on playing.
With my friend.
> *Will you pass me the crayons?*
> *Here you go!*
>> *Use your words, girls.*

We exchange smiles—
brilliant little eyes.
> *I am the mom, and this is my baby, Isabel.*
> *I'll be the dad. I'm a firefighter.*
>> *Guys! Use your words.*

I better not talk.
A book with a frosty face and golden hair.
> *Teacher, I don't understand.*
> *Can you help me read it?*
>> *Use your words, please.*

Now what?
How should I use them?
Aren't these *my* words coming out of *my* mouth?
Out of who I am?
Out of my short story?
These are the sounds I've known since birth.
These are the words of my mother.
Of my father.
Of my brother and sisters and grandparents who live in Skype.
They've been all I needed.

For everything.
Until today.
Until *you* came into *my* life.
So are they not words?
When I learn, I will look at you
and I will tell you
      Use my *words.*

FORTY-TWO

Privileged and Under

by Yvette A. Schnoeker-Shorb

First appeared in *The North Central Review* ("The Fate of Children" issue, fall 2003)

How recruit them
when college doesn't apply?
They are too intelligent to be led
into indoctrination, too busy
trying to survive
more than high school.

The seats set up by us in the library
remain predictably empty,
so I watch a group enter,
one teacher and five students—
no six, a maverick who wanders
to the window and waits to fly—
the others roam near the poetry section
like antelope around a cattle trough;
It's after school, and this field trip
is probably a form of punishment.

The maverick, a female
with carefully painted lips,
long, glossy hair (with
a blue streak down the middle),
and posture like a sigh,

is called by the teacher on guard duty,
"Angel, come join us—now!"

The angelic stray, wings poised
to take off, catches my eye as she passes,
knowing she'll never see me again,
whispers of her guardian,
"She's such a bitch" (pronounced
like the sand and surf place).
In that moment she teaches me
that the question isn't how to recruit,
but how to reach.

FORTY-THREE

The Goddess of Autumn

by Richard Levine

I sent a student home with a note,
"Your son refused to do today's
writing assignment: Write
an original myth to explain
how autumn began.

"Instead, he howled, threw his pen,
and crawled under desks, calling himself
autumn leaves in the wind. Please have him
complete the assignment at home,
and come to meet with me."

I didn't know his mother
was the Goddess of Autumn,
didn't know her complexion
raged through colors skin should
never know: phlegmy green,

rheumy yellow, orange, red,
gold. I knew the myths I read
to the class, about hair alive
with snakes, not knowing
about her chemo-clumps slithering

across the polished wooden floors
of their apartment, and turning
like tumbleweeds over the porcelain

prairies of the rank bathroom, or
how he finds them perched

like birds' nests on her pillow,
discarding and thinking of them
as death's fur. I knew the myths
I read to the class about people
being turned to stone with one

demon stare, not knowing
his face as a mirror of hers,
which has grown so strange
her gaze petrifies him. So what
could I make of her note:

Dear Teacher,
Autumn began the end,
when the Harvest Moon piped
of all things bountiful
through the broken horn

of Almathea, who like a single mom
nannied Zeus on Crete. That moon piped
all night and piped all day, and never
was its face bigger or brighter
than just before its death was born

and drove it mad with the pain
of shadows and waning, and then,
as every child's mother must,
it grew smaller and fainter
every night, though it never slept,

until it was no longer. Then,
even in the morning—and please
recognize how well you and every
mother's child knows this

to be true—even in the morning,
its vacant ghost-face is there,
staring at you, in every season
for the rest of your life. Yours
ever, The Goddess of Autumn.

PS—I'm dying, cut my kid some slack.

FORTY-FOUR

Reflection Questions for Part Five: Speaking Up and Talking Back

1. At the end of her poem "Three Spaces of Exclusion," V. Thandi Sulé refers to *colorblind liberalism, never-mind multiculturalism,* and *undermined egalitarianism.* What do you think these terms mean? Can you think of anything you have seen or experienced in schools that bring these terms to mind?

2. In "Starfish," Kyle "Guante" Tran Myhre explains that his job is "not to make a difference" but "to teach starfish to fly." What distinction is he making there?

3. Several of the poems and stories in this section describe how educators pushed back against school conditions they found untenable or repressive. What are some of the school conditions you would like to change in order to create more equitable and just learning environments for students?

Part Six

Advocacy and Solidarity

FORTY-FIVE

Connecting with Carlos: Reframing Pain into a Model of Resiliency and Activism

by Amy Vatne Bintliff

"Why did you finally talk to me after all these months? Why did you trust me with all of this?" I asked.

After a long pause, my seventeen-year-old student Carlos, who had sat in silence in my classroom for three months, quietly said, "You know pain. And you don't judge."

I followed him out of the room. His words hit me in my gut and took my breath away. I shut the door, enclosing myself in my classroom as my body began to shake. The sobs started from deep inside—they ripped at my core leaving me breathless. How could he know that I knew pain? I'd never told him about the weight I carried.

At that time, I was twenty-nine and had lived with an incurable chronic pain disease since the age of twelve. For over half my life, my right leg burned with a fire that no painkillers could stop. It was a constant battle, and at that point, I hadn't learned to cope with it gracefully. I ran from the pain by working long hours, pouring energy into my students, and evading questions from family and colleagues about my illness. There was anger when I stopped running. Dark spaces were filled with a sense of injustice that my childhood had changed when my own body had betrayed me and that the constant pain clung to me despite living a "good" life. That sense of injustice had shaped me, but had it enabled me to connect with students like Carlos?

Carlos's story was fraught with injustice, but in the beginning, I was removed from the details of his life. When he initially arrived in Minneapolis, at the alternative school where I taught, he carried the weight of his story in silence. His short, stocky frame, always dressed in navy blue, bore the evidence of gang activity. He would sit in the back of my language arts classroom, never speaking, but would nod when I spoke to him directly. His reticence stretched through October and November. It clung to me. It bothered me. I always had been proud that I could connect with all of my students—that they confided in and trusted me—but Carlos remained stoic, out of touch, unreachable. His cool stares were unnerving, but I continued to praise his work, ask him questions, smile, and engage with him.

Then one day in November, he walked up to me after class and asked, "Can I eat with you today?"

Surprised, I said, "Of course." I always had a room full of students during lunch, but I cleared the space for just the two of us that day.

As we sat with our lunches, Carlos began to tell me his story. He described being poor when he was little and what it felt like when his family couldn't find work. He shared his elementary school experiences; he always knew he was smart, but the teachers stuck him in a class with the "slow" kids because he primarily spoke Spanish. He recounted the day he was jumped into a gang on his twelfth birthday, beaten badly by his own family and the men who had helped raise him. As I asked how he felt about that, he shrugged. "I knew it was coming. It's my family history. It wasn't a choice."

As he spoke, I was filled with a myriad of emotions, from rage at the injustice he faced as a small child to shock that his young life contained so much grief. I could hear the tears in my voice as I quietly asked questions. I mostly sat in silence, listening. He finally spoke of the present. He shared his desire to graduate, to get out of the criminal life, to start again. But he described his choices as "limited" and his road paved with obstacles.

I could tell his words had been bottled for years and that the transmission of his pain was cathartic. But each word piled high on my spirit. I felt a great sense of responsibility for him but didn't know what I could do to help. His story was far out of the realm of my experience, yet I deeply connected with his reflection of being twelve years old and feeling that life was out of his control. Carlos's openness left me raw.

When our time ended and I asked him why he trusted me, his words—"You know pain. And you don't judge"—ricocheted through me. His sense that I could understand his pain, that I could feel it and relate to it, made me reconsider the path that led me to education and my commitment to social justice. Was I fighting against injustice because I felt the sting of it residing within my own pain? Did I choose to teach about human rights and social justice because I wanted justice to be reflected in my own life?

Carlos's observation was a catalyst forcing me to dig deeply into the psychology of my teaching, into the manner in which I connected with my students, and into the oppressions that I sought to fight. Was the very pain that tormented me a conduit that enabled me to empathize with my students? Perhaps my students felt it reflected in the stories and poems I selected, the topics we discussed, and the writings we shared together.

When I met Carlos, I didn't know what to do with his pain other than soak it up and withhold judgment. However, as Carlos and I continued to build our relationship, I became aware of an internal shift within my teaching. I began focusing on building the hurt, pain, and injustice of all my students' lives, as well as my own, into a model of resilience that celebrates pain but reframes it. I started teaching about oppression in my classes, identifying how it shaped literature and art and how people worked to fight against it. I began teaching about human rights and inviting authors and activists into our school to speak to my students about resiliency and making change.

Today, eight years later, the struggles shared in my classroom are reframed into narratives of activism. As my struggling readers share their frustrations with a system that left them unable to read, we reframe that pain into a collaborative classroom where students build structures that help them reach their goals. As my young females describe the pain of labels and stereotypes, we rebuild our identities through poetry and art that we share. These shifts build confidence in my students as they feel more in control of their lives and become more involved in activism within our school and community. And because teaching is a large part of my life, I am not left untouched personally—I no longer hide the evidence of my illness and have begun to accept that my own pain gifts me with insights and empathy in my work.

My personal story, though different from my students', weaves in and out of my interactions with them. It unifies us. It strengthens us until our shared experiences move us toward action and activism. Teachers hear a lot of stories like Carlos's. Every day in classrooms, teachers carefully and gently hold these stories in their hands and recognize them as great gifts. With reflective practice, we are able to shape those stories, and the pain that cloaks them, and help students rebuild the narratives into resiliency and activism.

Amy's student, Carlos, graduated from high school and received his diploma.

FORTY-SIX
Praise

by Julie Landsman

Baggy pants draped to the ground
flannel shirts and starter jackets that reach their wrists:
the kids are standing on the corner
waiting for love. They don't talk about it:
love's too tender for styling, the up-in-the-image.
White and black they play at anger,
sometimes succeed.
In the winter dawn of first hour at North High, Khalid
asks: *Where is the love?*
And for a moment they start to answer,
at home in my kitchen, under the front porch step,
Then they stop. Shake their heads
You crazy man. Talkin' about love.

Silence.

One dark eyed boy asks:
What I wanna know is, how come more people
Don't hang out with their grams much anymore? What is that, like is it history?

Khalid turns to us, later, as we sit around a table
in a seminar room that overlooks downtown streetlights,
lampposts draped for Christmas

He says, *the hallways are spiritual places,*
talks about how the kids are singing hip hop,
wearing Tommy Hilfiger clothes.

One boy is going into the army so he can send his check to his Moms.

One girl's grandmother is dying over on Queen Avenue, just off Plymouth.
This girl cannot bear to go to visit her now,
does not want to forget
the color and food, the music and love
that were there for years of her growing.
She refuses to replace memory with sour smell, wisps of hair
on balding head, loud breathing that almost stops.

Khalid asks: *"How come nobody ever talks about love anymore?"*

I say I think we are afraid of tenderness.
He laughs at that, says "give me a tender moment on the streets."
I say that one evening, in the middle of college teaching,
I found out that my mother had died.
A man from my class walked me to the parking lot,
singing spirituals in the fading April light
just to start you on your way home, he said, smiling,
leaning into the car window.

Khalid grins under his blue brimmed hat
says, *There is a story there.*

and praise, perhaps, for all the moments
in all the hallways, in all our lives
that come to that: someone knowing
the right song, the right question.
    Spiritual, you know.

And now,
        it is time to talk to the kids,
        earphones circling their heads, eyes
        closed to the beat. Now, oh now,
        it is time to talk some more about love

FORTY-SEVEN

Three Portraits

by Jehanne Beaton

Drawing from arts-based research, I have created fictional student portraits that evolve from quantitative, reductive representations to robust stories. The three students portrayed are Alex, Caroline, and Minerva. The portraits are fictionalized composites, grounded in details culled from years of classroom experience, observation, and work with diverse groups of secondary school students in settings like McKinley High School, the imagined context of my dissertation. Drawing on artifacts that schools like McKinley use to represent student learning, performance, and growth, each student portrait contains a series of documents: a report card, a standardized test report, a language assessment score, and a narrative written in third-person limited point of view. Each student's "file" composes a contradictory and complicated portrait. Partial stories of home and neighborhood sit beside generic teacher comments, such as "absent too often" and "good student." The reader has access to moments of educational and family history and language assessment scores, usually reserved for school personnel. Independently and together, the student artifacts create a portrait of the student that is intentionally incomplete.

In the creation of the student portraits, I merged detailed descriptions gathered over years of experience in diverse urban schools with composite findings from research focused on students in an attempt to render the complicatedness of each individual student and to demonstrate the multiple, intertwined, and fluid identities students carry into school. As an element in my larger dissertation work, the creation of multiple student portraits, as coconstructors of McKinley's changing context, might provide the reader with additional ways of seeing the unpredictable and complex experience of learning to teach in diverse urban schools. My hope is that the portraits generate questions and conversation about the student characters and, more broadly, students in schools. What might keep a student like Alex coming to school? If a student chooses not to continue, are there ways to interpret that choice as a better one for him? Does compliance make a good student? Do test scores? If not, what policies and practices do we have in place that counter that message? How valuable are grades and to whom are they valuable? What purpose do grades serve? The portraits offer up no neat and tidy answers.

My intention is to embed these student portraits in my larger dissertation work, focused on the felt experience of learning to teach in an urban school. The presence of these fictional students serves to tug the reader by the shirt as they theorize and render judgments about teaching, public education, teacher preparation, and urban classrooms. I imagine the students waving at the reader from the back of a classroom in another chapter or sneaking into a teacher's classroom to avoid a hall sweep. As the reader moves through the story of learning to teach in an urban high school, the student portraits supply the reader with a tap on the shoulder as a reminder: "Don't forget: I'm here."

BRIDLED: ALEX

Alex hates school. He bides his time. Watches the clock. Counts down to lunch, to the end of second hour, third, the end of the day. He shows up because his Nana Berta wants him to go. He sits there, as he has learned to do from years of sitting in desks, on line, hands folded, mouth closed. He contains himself. Silent, Alex keeps himself shut, sealed, stoic. He slides into his assigned desk in one room after another. He listens to them talk. Sometimes he hears them: *Get your notebook out. Essay due by Friday. Listen up.* Other times, he imagines their imperatives bouncing off of him like pinballs hitting those springing flaps, like raindrops off a metal roof. Impenetrable.

He remembers racing into Ms. B's room, hoping to be the first one in the kindergarten classroom. Like boxes of candy, cartons of books lined the window ledges, each with its own leveled number and colored bind-

MNHSTest

2013-2014
District: Midwest City Public School District
School: McKinley High School

Student's Name: ████, Alex   Student ID: ████   Grade: 10

Term/ Year	Grade	MIT (+/- Std Err)	Percentile Range	Term/ Year	Grade	MIT (+/- Std Err)	Percentile Range
FA13	10	237-**242**-247	99-**99**-99	FA 13	10	224-**229**-230	99-**99**-99

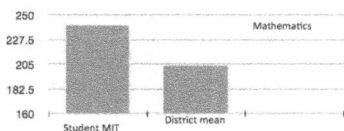

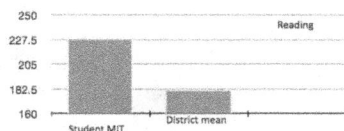

Problem solving	High	Measurement and geometry	High
Number sense	High	Statistics and probability	High
Computation	High	Algebra	High

Vocabulary	High	Grammar	High
Comprehension of literature	High	Analysis and evaluation of language and writing	High
Comprehension of informational texts	High		

MNHS Test

ing. Nana Berta had taught him to read before he ever got there. Alex pressed his grandmother's hand in his, pleading again and again to walk to the library, even if it was seven blocks from their apartment. They stopped to rest twice, three times on the way home, setting the overloaded bags of books on the sidewalk, so that Nana could rest her hands. Alex pulled the top book from the bag and sat cross-legged on the sidewalk and read.

The bridling started early on at school. *No blurting out your answers, Alex. Other children want a chance to answer questions, too. Please wait for the other children in your group. Don't read ahead. Not so fast*, the teacher would say. *Yes, that's the right answer; now go back and show your work.*

He remembers how much it hurt, the throb in his temple, the churn in his gut from waiting, trying to contain his ideas and questions. His thinking mutated, like electricity, like straight pins coursing through his body, searching for release. He bounced in his seat, kicked the bottom of the chair in front of him, again and again, until the kid called out, *Alex is bothering me.* Hopping to the pencil sharpener. Dancing on his way to the

First Quarter Report Card					
███ High School					
Name: Alex ███				Grade: 10 Date: ███	
Course	Per	Teacher	Grade	Comment 1	Comment 2
Health	1	███	F	41 – Frequently absent	
World History	2	███	D	83 – Poor work habits	31 – Not up to potential
English 10	3	███	D	83 – Poor work habits	
Welding	4	███	F	41 – Frequently absent	40 – Often tardy
Debate	5	███	A	08 – Outstanding student	27 – Very creative
Geometry	6	███	C-	05 – High test scores	83 – Poor work habits
Chemistry	7	███	F	42 – Unexcused absences	

First-Quarter Report Card

little bathroom in the corner of the kindergarten room. *In your seat, Alex. Keep your hands to yourself, Alex. You need to be quiet. Get yourself in line.*

At some point, the teachers lost patience. The words and questions that flew from his mouth before he was called on sent him out of the circle, to *timeout*, on the wall at recess, into the desk facing the corner, away from the other kids. His electrified body propelled him out the door to *isolation* in the teacher's classroom next door or for *a break* in the principal's office. Somewhere during that stretch, there was a social worker and some other woman who sat in his classroom, watching him, noting his kicks and wiggles, making hash marks for his blurts and bursts. There was a hot afternoon in a small office with lots of questions about being distracted and television and home.

I am a troublemaker, Alex told Nana when he came home from school. He buried himself in the stack of library books from their most recent trip, immersing himself in imagined basketball courts and space stations and superhero strategy sessions. *I don't feel so good*, he told his mom on

Monday mornings, and he stayed on the couch with Nana, keeping one eye on CNN or Montel, the other on the book in his lap. Then the moving started. Moving from one teacher to another, from one school to the next. Some were better than others: fewer worksheets and lines. The writhing electricity burned at the lining of his stomach, and he lay his head down on his desk. *He's not engaged. He works maybe 10 percent of the time. He doesn't listen.*

Then he took the tests. His third-grade teacher called Nana Berta first, then called his mom at work. *We want him to take them again. Sometimes the score can be a fluke.* Nana Berta hugged him hard, and they walked to the Dairy Queen for the biggest ice cream cone he had ever had. The next day, he took the tests again. No DQ this time. Instead, the third-grade teacher gave him more to do. A thick math book with pages of problems to do at home. Twenty spelling words instead of ten, plus he had to write all the definitions. In fourth grade, the teacher presented him with word finds and crossword puzzles. *Challenge work,* he explained. And timeouts. *Please don't correct me Alex.* If his work wasn't done, no recess. *There's no excuse for you not having it done, unless you're just lazy.*

He learned to keep his thoughts to himself around the other kids first. When Rafique and Cy and Eddie were talking about Pokémon and Nintendo and football at lunch, he found ways to contribute to their conversations without using words like *hypothetically* or *paucity* or *carcass*, words that crystalized meaning in books. It only took one, *Quit-using-big-words-ya-know-it-all,* and Alex left the words on the page. In elementary school he rattled off stats for Kobe Bryant and Kevin Garnett. By middle school, it was kung fu movies, *Grand Theft Auto,* and cigarettes.

Nana Berta was sick then, and his mom bit at her lip every time she thought about what it would mean to have a teenage boy in the house by herself, a boy whose teachers called him *impulsive* and *spacey* and *noncompliant.* She enrolled him in a new charter school when Alex was in seventh grade. Its brochures promised a no-excuses college preparation program and structure in a 7–5 school day. She borrowed a car from her girlfriend and drove him to a suburban mall for the required uniform of khaki pants and navy shirts. Alex lasted three months. The teachers marched them in lines from class to class, insisted on silent hand signals to leave their desks, to sharpen their pencils, to throw away trash, to return a book to the cupboard. Alex received detention again and again for slouching, for not tracking the reading teacher, for untucking his shirt.

At some point, it was a game. What rule could he violate, and how long would it take them to catch him? Then Alex stopped talking altogether. His mother only heard his voice when he read out loud to Nana Berta as she lay in bed. *Your son is angry*, his teachers said at his exit conference. *You might look into getting a diagnosis.*

Alex skipped across three different middle schools during eighth grade, finally landing at McKinley as a freshman. At that point, he had been in truancy court twice, and a thick file followed him to school.

But Alex shows up at McKinley because Nana Berta wants him to. He slides into his assigned desk in one class after another, and he stays silent. At home he reads and rereads DuBois, Mumia Abu Jamal, and Malcolm X. Sometimes he even brings a copy to school and reads it in class while the teachers lecture. They mostly don't care so long as he's quiet. Sometimes he does the work they ask him to. Other times not. Pretty much any kid will ask him for a smoke in the hallway, and he will always oblige, behind a locker or in a still back stairwell.

But in debate, his fourth-hour class, he can run. Two weeks into the semester, Ms. Altoonian handed him a book on the prison industrial complex and told him he could take it home. *Just return it when you're done.* He finished it within the week. After that it was a graphic novel about race and the school-to-prison pipeline. He scanned her classroom, looking for a catch, a sign that she wasn't for real. *What do you think?* She asked him one day, when he showed up a few minutes early and the room was still empty. *Good*, he said, and he set the book on her desk. *What's next?* He asked.

You tell me.

MCKINLEY'S IT: CAROLINE

When Caroline first heard about McKinley, she was in third grade.

Caroline always thought her cousin Becca was perfect. Even after Becca got pregnant, she was perfect to Caroline. Becca went to McKinley High, which was a long walk across the footbridge that hung over the freeway, and after school, Becca came over to Caroline's house. *It's closer*, Becca explained. *Your house is on my way home.* When Caroline and her twin younger sisters, Caty and Carly, got home from Madison Elementary, Becca would be there and would stay with the girls until her mom got home. Sometimes the girls took out the game of Sorry! or, if the twins insisted, Candyland, and the four played board games until Carly started crying because she was losing or Caroline got sick of it. But Becca never quit the game.

Other times, Becca would let her cousins play with her hair. Caty and Carly would run to the bathroom, brushes and combs spilling out of drawers, the girls gathering all colors of bows and barrettes, all of which would end up perched in Becca's auburn hair. While the girls argued over which brush to use or exactly where to place a bobby pin, Becca talked on the phone, the spiral cord stretching from the kitchen into the den. Caroline assumed she was talking to boys. A boy. Many boys. Maybe a different boy each day, like teenage girls did in all the books and on the Nickelodeon shows she watched. In between phone calls, Becca made hot dogs in the microwave or dumped a bag of Doritos from the corner store into a bowl. The twins carried the bowl to the den, each of them sitting on pillows in front of the TV, snacking while Becca did her homework at the kitchen table. Big heavy textbooks open, Becca blew through it. She had it done in no time flat. And then she would stuff the textbook

	2013-2014
	District: Midwest City Public School District
	School: McKinley High School

Student's Name: ▉▉▉, Caroline   Student ID: ▉▉▉   Grade: 10

Term/Year	Grade	MIT (+/- Std Err)	Percentile Range	Term/Year	Grade	MIT (+/- Std Err)	Percentile Range
FA13	10	207-212-217	72-76-83	FA 13	10	196-201-206	84-87-93

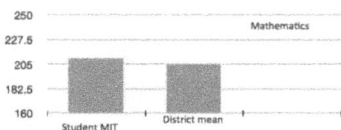

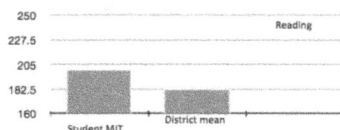

Problem solving	Mid	Measurement and geometry	Mid
Number sense	High	Statistics and probability	High
Computation	Mid	Algebra	Mid

Vocabulary	High	Grammar	Mid
Comprehension of literature	High	Analysis and evaluation of language and writing	High
Comprehension of informational texts	Mid		

MNHS Test

back in her backpack and drink a glass of water, her knees pulled up on the edge of the couch.

Sometimes Becca would stay for supper, but then Caroline's mom would make her go home. *It's no big deal*, Becca always said. But every night, Caroline asked her mom, *Could Becca stay? Just a while longer? Overnight? 'Til breakfast? Can Dad drive her home later?* To Caroline, it just seemed like Becca didn't want to go home anyway. Most times, Becca left before Caroline's mom lost her patience and yelled loud enough to make the curtains curl. Caroline would run to her room and cry, watching Becca from her bedroom window. The dark winter sky would be closing in, and Becca would pull her jacket tight around her as she walked in the direction of her house.

Becca got pregnant at the end of her sophomore year at McKinley, and her parents kicked her out. That's when she came to stay with Caroline, Caty, and Carly. At Thanksgiving dinner, Becca, all nervous, bounced

First Quarter Report Card					
██████ High School					
Name: Caroline ██████				Grade: 10	
				Date: ████████	
Course	Per	Teacher	Grade	Comment 1	Comment 2
English 10	1	████████	B	20 – Very cooperative	10 – Good written work
World History	2	████████	B	06 – Excellent homework	36 – Low participation
Chemistry	3	████	C	20 – Very cooperative	31 – Not up to potential
P.E.	4	█████	D	36 – Low participation	66 – Needs gym clothes
Geometry	5	████	B	20 – Very cooperative	11 – Good daily work
Choir	6	███████	C+	70 – Missed performance	
French	7	████	A	23 – Working to ability	25 – Good participation

First-Quarter Report Card

baby Jordan in her arms like he had a bug on his onesie and she was trying to shake it off. Right there at the table in front of everyone, even Caty and Carly, Becca's dad blamed it on the blacks at McKinley. This never ever made any sense to Caroline. Jordan, who woke up crying loud as ever, either from the bouncing or the yelling, looked just as white as the rest of the family.

Becca stayed with Caroline's family for three years. Caroline's parents moved a second bed and a crib into Caroline's room. When Jordan was three, Becca found a job that would take someone without a high school diploma. She also moved in with her boyfriend. Dustin. *Total loser,* Caroline's mom said. Caroline's mom still helps with Jordan. She picks him up from Madison Elementary, down the street, and walks him to her house. Then she leaves for work, and Caroline watches him once she gets home from McKinley. He's like a little brother and a son, even though he's a cousin.

When Caroline told her parents she wanted to go to McKinley for high school, they gave each other their prune-faced concerned looks. Then they set about learning everything they could about the school. They went to both open houses. They took turns showing up for tours and sitting down with the school counselors. Her father even sat in on a history class. They had visited McKinley when Becca was there. During Becca's two years there, they talked to the teachers and social worker to make sure she got into the program for teen moms and that Jordan got into the daycare, located right there in the school.

Caroline's mom tried to convince her daughter to attend Martin Luther Christian Academy. *It's a very nice school, Caroline. You'll get a good education.* Then when Caroline's father lost his job, the private school was less of an option. Neither the odd jobs he landed nor the position his wife held as a nurse's aide at the senior center offered health insurance. This stress piled on top of the years when they housed and cared for Becca and Jordan. It took a toll on their finances, but her dad refused to put Becca out. *No way in hell is a niece of mine living in a shelter.* And Becca's parents refused to let her come home. They still won't see Jordan. Caroline's parents simply haven't saved all that much. So, Caroline knows, McKinley's it. *It's close, just right over the freeway.* Some of the kids from the neighborhood go there, so she will know a few people when she starts. Becca always says the schoolwork will be easy for Caroline. *I never did have much homework.*

Caroline's parents worry, though. Now that she's there, they never miss conferences and always sign all the letters that come home from McKinley so that they go back the very next day. They call the main office in a heartbeat if they haven't heard about when report cards are coming home. When it comes to McKinley and Caroline, they pay close attention.

But it's fine. The teachers are nice, and Caroline has made a couple of good friends. Caroline does her homework at the kitchen table while Jordan watches TV or plays in the backyard. Caty and Carly come home from middle school late because both of them are involved in all sorts of after-school sports. Caroline's parents are looking into a suburban high school for the twins. It's further away, but it has better athletic programs than McKinley. It's on the bus line, so it's not that far. And they can go together, which makes a difference.

Looks like Caroline will have McKinley all to herself.

GOOD STUDENT: MINERVA

Minerva's papi drops her off on that first day of kindergarten. She doesn't speak English. Not a word. They've been in the country two weeks. And nobody at the school speaks Spanish, but Papi has heard from the other roofers he works with that it's a good school. And that's what matters.

The kindergarten teacher, Ms. Worth, smiles a lot and gently touches Minerva's arm, motioning with her hands to come near her, to work with this smiling blond girl who doesn't stop talking. Minerva cries in Spanish. *Where is my papi? When is he coming back? Is he coming back at all?*

All Minerva can remember is that there is this white woman, maybe one of the other kids' moms. She is there, and she knows some Spanish. Her Spanish sounds funny, but it's just enough to get the girl to stop crying. She sits on the floor with the girl and asks in Spanish, *Do you know your numbers?* Minerva recites her numbers in soft Spanish, and the volunteer mom says them back to Minerva in English. Even on that first day, Minerva knows the lady wants her to repeat the English words back at her. Minerva speaks in numbers and then letters, in both Spanish and English. She stumbles, even giggles, over the English names of animals and objects in the classroom. Minerva is almost okay. Her nose is no longer stuffed, her tears have stopped. And then the volunteer mom has to leave. *I have to go to work,* she says to Minerva in Spanish, and then

2013-2014
District: Midwest City Public School District
School: McKinley High School

Student's Name: ████, Minerva   Student ID: ████   Grade: 9

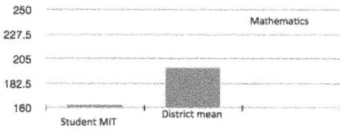

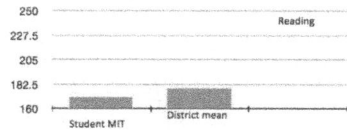

Term/Year	Grade	MIT (+/- Std Err)	Percentile Range	Term/Year	Grade	MIT (+/- Std Err)	Percentile Range
FA13	9	159-**164**-169	16-**20**-24	FA 13	9	167-**172**-177	36-**40**-44

Problem solving	Low	Measurement and geometry	Low
Number sense	Low	Statistics and probability	Low
Computation	Mid	Algebra	Low

Vocabulary	Low	Grammar	Low
Comprehension of literature	Low	Analysis and evaluation of language and writing	Low
Comprehension of informational texts	Low		

MNHS Test

Minerva starts crying again. Minerva cries and cries until her head hurts and the skin above her upper lip is raw from wiping it. She cries until the teacher walks her to the office at the end of the day. Papi is there, and Minerva cries some more.

All through elementary school, Minerva does what the teachers ask. She is quiet in class. She goes with the ESL teacher when she is supposed to and works on her letter sounds. She collects English words at school, Spanish words at home. As she gets older, she sometimes wonders if she should tell her teachers that the work is too easy, too boring. When her test scores come back, she thinks, *I better not*. The teachers give Minerva less than the other kids. Thinner books with bigger words. Her worksheets have sections crossed off. Minerva completes the parts the teacher marks yellow, the problems circled in red. Minerva prides herself on her handwriting. She loves practicing her cursive letters, writing swirly capital *E*s and lowercase *z*s over and over again. Minerva always sits in the front of the class when the teacher reads aloud the day's story. Minerva always keeps her hands in her lap.

Name: Minerva ███████		Date administered: █████
Grade 9	Home Language: Spanish	
Language Domain	Scale Score (Possible 100-600)	Proficiency Level (possible 1.0-6.0)
Speaking	307	4.2
Listening	404	4.9
Writing	410	4.8
Reading	385	4.7
Oral Language^A	387	4.6
Literacy^B	397	4.8
Overall Score^C (Composite)	393	4.6

A – Oral Language = 50% Listening + 50% Speaking

B – Literacy = 50% Reading + 50% Writing

C – Overall Score = 35% Reading + 35% Writing +15% Listening + 15% Speaking

Good Student: Minerva

In seventh grade, Minerva's classes are full of other Mexican kids. A few Somali and Ethiopian kids are there, too. The worksheets are different from the ones the American kids get but the same for all of the ESL kids, no matter what language is spoken at home.

Minerva carries her lunch up three flights of stairs every day during middle school. She, along with Marta, Grizelda, Ana, and Luz, leave the cafeteria and eat their lunches in Ms. Ochoa's classroom. Ms. Ochoa is the ESL teacher. Twice a week, Minerva stays after school, sometimes for as much as two hours, to get help from Ms. Ochoa on her work. Her girlfriends do, too, all except Ana, who has to go home and care for her younger siblings so her dad can sleep before he heads for work. Even though Ms. Ochoa says her family is from Puerto Rico (but her Spanish isn't that good), she talks to Minerva and her friends about being Hispanic and staying in school. She lets them speak Spanish in class, even when they are working on their language arts assignments, even when they

First Quarter Report Card					
███ High School					
Name: Minerva ███				Grade: 9	
				Date: ███	
Course	Per	Teacher	Grade	Comment 1	Comment 2
Geography	1	███	B	39 – Good attendance	96 – Poor writing skill
English 9	2	███	B	36 – Low participation	19 – Good attitude
French	3	███	C	20 – Very cooperative	23 – Working to ability
P.E.	4	███	D	36 – Low participation	66 – Needs gym clothes
Biology 9	5	███	B	20 – Very cooperative	11 – Good daily work
Algebra I	6	███	C+	12 – Low test scores	97 – Needs more ESL
Art	7	███	A	11 – Good Daily work	

First-Quarter Report Card

have to write in English. Even when she doesn't entirely know what they are saying. *You kids! Your Spanish is too fast for me!*

In Minnesota history, the teacher stands at the overhead projector and uncovers an outline. He lowers the paper and reveals one line for the students to copy and then the next. One line, then the next. Minerva and her classmates read it and write it in their social studies notebooks. Every day, that is the task: *Copy the outline in your notebooks. No talking.* While the students write, the teacher tells stories about how Minnesota became a state or about James J. Hill and the railroad, *with a Chinaman under every rail tie.* After a week or two of outlines and stories, the students write a paper about it. For Minerva and Grizelda and Marta, the teacher ushers them to the small circular table in the back of the room. He has a paper already written. *Just copy it,* he tells them. *Add anything you like.* The girls look at each other and stay quiet. They write his words on their papers. Exactly. Minerva, Grizelda, and Marta each receive an A in Minnesota history. Minerva's report card says, *Good student.*

FORTY-EIGHT

Willie Alexander

by Thomas Turman

The phone rang just as I was about to leave my office and go across campus to one of the college's professional development seminars. We do these seminars the week before classes begin, so I wondered who would be calling.

"Is this T. L. Turman?" a tired and gruff voice demanded.

"Yes."

"Are you the department chair of the architecture department at Laney?"

"Yes, who is this?"

"I'm Devon Mitchell, Oakland Office of State Corrections. I'm Willie Alexander's probation officer," he said, with the air of a partner in crime.

I hadn't seen any students yet for the coming semester, and because I didn't recognize the name, I said, "How can I help you?"

"Damn! He hasn't *talked* to you yet?" he shouted, "I *told* him to get to you this week. Damn!" He was getting louder and louder as he rambled on. He was frustrated, angry, and taking it out on me. He must have realized what he was doing. There was a pause, and then he continued in a softer tone, "Sorry, Willie's one of my cases. He told me he was interested in drafting and that he was going to go to Laney. I haven't heard from him since."

"Well, classes don't start until next week, so there is still time for him to sign up."

"Let me fill you in, Mr. Turman. Willie is on probation for two years, and a condition of his probation is that he prepares for and then gets a job. He has to stay away from the old crowd in East Oakland, go to school, and get a job, or he goes back in for the rest of his sentence."

Curious, I asked, "What did he do?"

"Can't divulge that to you at this time. If he shows up to your class, you and I will have to arrange a method for me to monitor his progress. Sorry to spring this on you, but I thought he had already signed up. I'm too much of an optimist I guess."

"Well, you have to be to stay at the job you've got. I'm an optimist, too, so how do I get in touch with you when he shows up?"

"If he attends your class, he is required to tell you of his probation conditions, and he will give you a form with my number on it. This form is a kind of a contract between him, you, and me. Good luck, and keep in touch." The line went dead.

I forgot about this conversation until a week later, when classes began. At the end of the first day, I was gathering up all the extra handouts, textbooks, and roll sheets and heading for my office, when I looked up to see a student still sitting at his desk. "You waiting for me?" I asked.

I motioned him to follow me into my office, a small space surrounded by architectural models, and gestured for him to sit down.

He sat down, but instead of looking at me, he began studying the models. This gave me a chance to put all my stuff down and study him. He was tall, maybe 6'4", thin and gaunt looking. His scraggly hair and beard gave him a scarecrow appearance. The dark skin showing below his shirtsleeves bore tattoos I couldn't read, and he wore bright yellow tennis shoes. Finally, he turned and looked at me with deep-set eyes.

"I'm Willie Alexander. You can call me Willie. Mitchell told me he already talked to you."

"Yeah, he did." I paused, not wanting to get into the forms, probation, and such just yet. I studied him for a few seconds and then asked one of my standard questions of first-semester students, "What do you want to do with these classes, Willie? Where do you want to go with what we offer here?"

He relaxed in the stiff chair and seemed relieved that I didn't jump right into the legal stuff. "See all this?" he said, as he waved his hand over the models next to him. "I want to do this. I want to draw, make models, and design," he began to talk faster. "I used to make models when I was a kid, and draw, too." His eyes lit up, and I knew he was in the right place.

I described the two-year program we have at the community college and gave him some information on transferring to four- or five-year colleges. This was my standard introduction talk to students who ask for career counseling.

He just stared at me when I finished and then said slowly, "I didn't finish the seventh grade, T."

He'd apparently decided to call me *T*. It either stood for *teacher* or *Turman*. Either way, if this nickname relaxed him, it was OK with me.

I shrugged and said, "I've seen worse. Let's just see how it goes, OK?" Now it was his turn to shrug.

We got Devon Mitchell's paperwork out of the way, and I assured Willie that the information was confidential. No one else needed to know. He studied me intently for a few seconds, nodded, and left.

Willie excelled in my classes. He had great critical insights as we discussed other students' work. He was one of those natural class leaders. Even when I saw him drumming with other musicians in the college square in front of the student union building, he stood out in his yellow shoes.

Each week, I'd get this gruff call with no pleasantries that began, "This is Mitchell. You got any problems with Willie Alexander?" He was always in a rush due to his enormous caseload.

I'd tell Mitchell that Willie was doing great and there were no problems.

One day a student ran into the drafting room and shouted, "Mr. T, did you tell that guy he could take books from your office?" He was pointing out the window to a man hurrying away with an armload of my books.

"No," I said and took off after the thief. I ran through the door and was about ten yards behind the book-nabber near a concrete staircase, when a flash of scraggly hair and yellow shoes came from the robber's right, cutting his legs out from under him. The books went flying, and Willie was on the guy, his fighting fist ready to strike. I reached him just in time, huffing and puffing. He looked at me, and I just shook my head. *No.* Willie stared long and hard at me and then at the guy on the ground. He jerked the guy up and tossed him down the stairs. We began picking up my books. When we got the books back into my office, he said, "Don't tell Mitchell. It'll just be a lot of paperwork for everybody."

Willie missed class only once and called me at home to admit that he'd been hanging out with his old crowd. He said he was sorry and begged to keep this probation violation from Mitchell. We agreed to keep it between us with the agreement that it would be the only time.

Willie loved to draw. He told me he wanted his own company so he could draw all day and listen to music. I could see his absolute love for drafting and guided him toward computer-aided drawing. He took two classes, saw the advantage, but wanted to go back to drawing with a pencil. I was secretly proud, as I love to draw with the "old tools," too. His main worry was that without degrees he wouldn't have "those letters" to put after his name. "Look at Mitchell's card," he'd say, "impressive bunch of letters, T." I told him the letters don't always mean a lot and that we'd figure something out.

Willie stayed with our department for the full two years, taking every class we offered, and then some. He did very well, and Mitchell called less and less. He rejected the idea of transferring to one of the architectural programs at the state university and graduated from Laney with an associate of arts degree in architecture/engineering.

A few weeks after our graduation ceremonies, I was walking to a coffee shop with the dean of the University of California's architecture program. Willie came striding up to us, yellow shoes flapping on the sidewalk, and thrust out a business card. The dean took a fearful step backward. "I'm in business, T. What do you think?" I took the brown card. In black ink, it said,

William Alexander, Ex. C.
Designer, Draftsman, Drummer
Call for appointment
(510) 414-3134

I smiled, and stuck out my hand to shake his. He pushed my hand aside, wrapped me in a big hug, and then continued to flap on down the street. I had tears in my eyes and couldn't speak.

The dean waited for me to gain my composure, and when Willie was far enough away, he whispered, "What does *Ex. C.* mean?"

I gripped the card tightly, turned to watch the yellow shoes of this ex-convict disappear, and said, "Excellent citizen."

FORTY-NINE

Knowledge as a Function of Freedom

by Toby Jenkins

Breaking Free

With a sign on his chest and conviction in his heart, he stands
He's been sitting way too long
His feet are restless
Got a nagging little itch to stick and kick his big toe in the trenches
Sick and tired of the seat belt of oppression that holds him on a ride
He doesn't want to take
He's ready to break free
So he
Clicks, cuts, and comes out of those straps
And takes a chance
No doubt he might crash
But he'll try his best to hold onto the dash
Because it's worth it
He deserves it
He's earned it
He's just way too tired to sit
So worn out that all he can do is stand
Way too exhausted . . . so he walks
Got that type of fever that burns so hot
You've got to get up
Forget the chair, Get out of the bed
He'd rather take to the pavement instead
And stand and shout and holler and scream
"I am a man" . . . listen to me

Respect me
Believe in me
Care about me
Revere me
Appreciate me
Adore me
Love me
And I do
I see beauty in what others call ugly
I see vulnerability where others see thug
I see intelligence where others see hustler
When others see you as threatening I see you as kind
I love the complexity and depth of your mind
The weight of your experience
The sensitivity of your heart's design
It gives me pause
Makes me stand in awe
Makes me draw
Stick figures
Imagining just how far
You can go in life
All that you can do just in spite
All you can give when you channel all of your might
I'm talking about real love here
Mama love
Daughter love
Sister love
Family love
Teacher love
Preacher love
Mentor love
Stranger just smiling at you kind of love
I'm talking this is why I work so hard kind of love
I mean making a difference kind of love
Changing lives and futures kind of love
And I'm willing to love you in all of the spaces that you engage the process of
finding yourself
I love you as a laborer
I love you as a prisoner
I love you as a scholar
I love you as a brother
I love you as a father
I love you as a neighbor

In this project I engage in love-based work

LEARNING INSIDE THE EXPERIENCE

Several years ago, I created a graduate course focused on the social issues confronting men of color. In particular, I sought to examine the school-to-prison pipeline, the role of education in contributing to or helping to address the problem, and the broader social and cultural issues that also play a role. However, as an educator, I personally needed it to be more than another seminar in which we reviewed relevant literature, wrote research papers, and chose to safely confront an issue that was affecting real people from the tucked-away confines of the campus gates. It seemed that men of color weren't the only ones imprisoned. In many ways, as scholars (teachers and learners), we were barred from the communities we study by the boundaries and gates of campus. So I decided that we needed to hold this course inside of the state prison. We needed to interact with more than literature, research, and our own opinions—we needed the wealth of knowledge and experience from the men who were currently a part of the criminal justice system. This is how the project "Breaking Bread" was born. I called the course "Breaking Bread" because in many ways I see the sharing of knowledge as soul food. I sought for our conversations to be modeled in the spirit of the type of incredible dialogue that occurs when communities come together in a spirit of love and communion over food. In this case, our "food" would be books, articles, and poetry. What we found was a community of young men who were, in fact, hungry for knowledge.

I joined thirteen graduate students with fifteen inmates. Once a week, we visited the prison and held our seminar there. Creating a course of this nature takes a lot of work, planning, and time: transportation, security clearances, prison review of course materials, training of students on allowed conduct with inmates, and so on. There was a long list of administrative details that had to be addressed. I also wanted to document the learning that took place in this experience for any future research projects. I secured informed consent from all participants to record our sessions and conversations so that I could write about what took place during each class session. After several weeks of administrative planning, we were ready to begin.

I started the course by having two sessions exclusively with the college students on campus. During these orientation sessions, we covered such issues as recidivism, education programs in prisons, stereotypes, prejudices, goals, and reasons for taking this course. During our preprison conversations, the students expressed genuine enthusiasm about the upcoming experience.

Chavez was an African American male doctoral student who grew up with friends who wound up in jail. His interest in the course came from his belief that he wasn't that different from some of the men who wind up in prison. "My friends were good guys. They made different life decisions, but they aren't that far off from a black male in my position." A few decisions away from a PhD. Imagine what that means. Chavez had few reservations about interacting with the inmates. He saw the course as an opportunity to be a part of a "bigger public."

Another student, Megan, was completing a master's degree in genetics. For her, this course offered an opportunity that was culturally beneficial: "I want to gain the experience of what it's like being around people who appear to be different than me. I think that, once we start learning, it will be the case that we are all just students trying to learn from each other. I've been guilty of playing into stereotypes about prison before. The only way for me to deal with those beliefs is to challenge myself to really humble myself and learn from the inmates."

Jehnel, a nontraditional undergraduate student, worked hard to secure permission to take this course. Jehnel was thirty-nine, finishing her senior year as a liberal arts major. She had spent many years working as an officer in a correctional facility in New York. She hadn't seen an experience like this come up in the course offerings since she went back to college. She came from a different place of having already experienced the culture of prison and worked with inmates. With this past experience came a commitment to them: "I started out with an attitude. I hated the inmates. The academy makes you think they are dehumanized, but overall, people who are incarcerated are smart; they just made bad choices. Or they might have had limited options. They are forced to make some of the decisions they make because of the way society is structured for men of color. A lot of them don't want to be like that. If they had more options, they wouldn't be where they are. I know that now after my African American studies and women's studies classes. I'm excited to have a class where we look at these social issues along with the men in prison. Even just being in the prison makes the experience more real."

Our Visits

Our first ride to the prison was a quiet one. I have taken college students in vans to a lot of places, and never has the ride been quiet. At first I thought, "Well these are graduate students, not undergrads. The energy level is different." But after glancing at a few faces, I realized some of them were just scared. I prodded Endeara, the student sitting directly behind me. She's normally a talker, and even she was dead quiet. She admitted, "I don't really know what to expect. I know we went over stuff, but I don't want to judge. I'm just preparing myself mentally. I don't want to offend anyone." That's fair. Regardless of the kind of community of difference in which we are immersing students, and no matter how much we orient, teach, and prepare them for the experience, truly being ready is a personal, mental, and meditative experience. It's a "get your mind right" type of moment. So I let them have it.

We entered the facility, each of us was searched, and then we went through several barred and electronically locked doors to get to the common area where our class would take place. By this time, the students had warmed up and channeled their energy into interacting with our guest speaker. I was able to gain funding to invite the author of one of the books we were going to read to join us to help kick off the first session with a book talk. Kevin Powell is a longtime community organizer and social activist. He often lectures on college campuses, but he was particularly thrilled about the nature of this experience. His excitement was contagious, and the group was becoming calm and relaxed.

Before the inmates entered, all of us, including Kevin, were confronted with the conflicting realities of prison with our personal values of community, love, and uplift. We were asked to refrain from shaking hands with or hugging any of the inmates. It would result in them automatically having to endure a strip search once we left. If the inmate initiated a handshake, that was fine as it communicates that he would rather have the social exchange and is willing to endure the demeaning nature of the strip search. But they asked that we didn't initiate it and force that search experience on any inmate. We struggled with this. To shake someone's hand is a show of respect. To hug is a show of brotherhood, sisterhood, and solidarity. We were already self-conscious about the inmates judging us as being privileged or thinking that we believed ourselves to be better than them, but we obliged. We shook the hands that were offered and greeted everyone else warmly.

Using his book *Who's Gonna Take the Weight?* as a foundation, Kevin spoke with all of us openly about his personal experiences growing up in New Jersey with no father, struggling financially, and dealing with issues of anger, misogyny, and poor decisions. Like Chavez, he didn't see himself as that much different than many of the men who sat before him. He just learned how to deal with his issues differently. He decided to change. He noted:

> You can be in prison, but prison doesn't have to be in you. You can't control or change what happened in your past. But you can control your future. The society we live in programs us to hate ourselves, to hate our neighborhoods. So we destroy them. We're being trained but not being educated; we self-sabotage ourselves by not getting an education. If we don't begin to turn our lives around, no one is going to do it for us.

Maurice, a young man serving seven years, spoke up:

> I've learned a lot in prison. You know, he is right. You can be dangerous when you're ignorant and don't know anything.

Another inmate, Samir, attended Temple University for four years before going to prison. He had words of warning for the students:

> Learn things while in college. But learn more than what they teach you. You have no idea how fortunate you are that you get to spend most of your time just learning. This book. It speaks to the powerlessness of black people. It speaks to our powerlessness.

At this point, I jump in with a critical challenge for Samir:

> There might be something else to be learned from this book. For me it was a call for us to be honest with ourselves in our own lives. He's speaking against the essentialism that says if you're a man you have to be this and you have to do that. The reality is that we all need to check ourselves.

Samir considers it, agrees, and pushes further:

> Yeah you're right. Like he talks about sexism. It's the patriarchal system set in place in America that makes sexism have a hold on our psyche. Sexism comes from a system that goes beyond us. It teaches us to think that men can't be sensitive. This country is based on vertical

relationships and objectification. That's what I'm saying about power-lessness. Until you are truly educated, you don't even realize who has the power—who decided that this is the way we're supposed to think.

And I answer:

Yes, it really is an issue of power and respect. We don't just need an education; we need a critical education—a relevant one.

I share this full exchange here because this is the type of conversation we expect in a college classroom. I have taught a lot of classes, but rarely do I find myself discussing patriarchy and objectification so intensely on the first day. I cringe when I hear folks say that young black men don't want to learn. In my educational work, I have seen otherwise, and my view has been from prisons, street corners, open mics, and hip-hop cyphers, not just classrooms.

Over the course of the semester, the entire group enjoyed much of this debate, exchange, and shared learning. After each session, I would take the college students to dinner, where we would debrief and process the experience. Their reflections affirmed the multiple layers of benefit from this experience. Endeara shared that her preconceived notions were completely proven wrong. She looked back at her nervousness in the beginning and laughed, "Some of them feel like people from home. There was something familiar about them. I mean they were self-confident, socially aware, and really intelligent. I felt pressured to read and make sure I was prepared for class each week." Jehnel echoed the feelings she brought into the experience: "Like I said before, they're very knowledgeable. Some of the students got to see that not everyone that goes to jail is illiterate or ignorant. This has taught me not to condemn even more. I've learned to appreciate the inmates."

We ended our sessions by putting the books and scholarship aside and focusing on poetry and spoken word. I am a poet, and poetry has always been a significant part of my family foundation. Our family showed love and support through poetry. When I was growing up, every Saturday we had a family talent show, and everyone had to recite a poem. And so, whenever I want to bring a sense of community, family, and love into a space, I go to poetry. One of the things that I love about hip hop and spoken word in our contemporary society is that they are among the few spaces that actually listens to young, disenfranchised people. In hip-hop culture, a cypher is a circle in which everyone takes their turn sharing. While one person is sharing, the circle remains tight, and everyone listens intently. So for our closing session, we formed a cypher, and everyone shared. Samir commenced the experience by repeating, "Let the circle be unbroken," until we were all centered and focused in our cypher. What the men in the prison brought to this closing session were poems that ultimately shared more about their lives, experiences, feelings, and emotions. Curtis was twenty-five years old and had been on a college football scholarship before he was imprisoned. In his poem he shared that there was a time when he thought he had tough decisions to make in college. He was wrong. He was now facing a choice to accept a plea and serve six to twelve more years or fight his case with the possibility of winning and going free or losing and being sentenced to life in prison. Poetry is how he has been processing these choices. Christopher, also known as "Logic," had been looking forward to the arts session all semester. He raps, writes poetry, and break dances. As he got up to share his work, he started by saying, "Me being here right now is a blessing."

And ultimately, that is how I felt as I reflected on this course as the instructor. There was so much involved here coordinating logistics; planning course content; booking guest speakers; navigating two different populations of students and making sure each of them never left bruised or hurt; processing out the personal, intellectual, and social development that students were getting each week; and caring for my own emotional health in the process. Learning some of the inmates' stories deeply affected me, and I decided that, to facilitate the experience, I needed to build in weekly therapy sessions for myself to create a space for me to deal with the experience, not just as an educator, but also as a person who deeply loves and sincerely wants to help people. What I seek in all of my work is more than a learning experience for students. I am honestly looking to create something spiritual: self-awareness, contemplation, finding life purpose, giving of self, and valuing our interconnectedness. My goal is not to simply create courses but to create blessings—experiences that bless both my students and myself with life-changing moments.

FIFTY

School Talk

by Stacy Amaral

My name is Arlene Shapiro, and I'm a retired school secretary. I was at one school for almost thirty years and got to know many parents and neighbors. Even after I retired, I subbed for other secretaries, so take it from me, I know what I'm talking about. I have many stories to tell.

Don't be fooled—schools are fine breeding grounds for stories of all kinds: romances, mysteries, short stories, poems even. I've seen teachers fall in love with each other and almost come to blows. I guess one would say that I'm a frustrated writer. In my day, girls (and we were all 'girls' back then) were often secretaries. Most days, and depending on the principal, the work was just fine for me. There were a couple of those principals, though, who were just not up for the job. You have to wonder how they got there, but then you don't need to wonder for too long. I'll tell you how. It was politics, yes. Politics and whom you knew.

Well, to the point: Schools have their own language, and if you don't know it, as the kids say, you are screwed. I'd like to share with you what I mean by this—just a few things I witnessed.

1. THE MISSILE

Years ago, a boy who lived across the street from the school started first grade with us. He had gone to kindergarten at a neighborhood daycare center in September of that year. One day, right before dismissal, the father of the boy came in with his son. "I was waiting for the bell to ring," said the father, "so I could watch out for him, but before I heard the bell there was a banging on the door."

Then he said that, when he opened the door, he saw his boy flustered, sweaty, and panting in front of him.

"So I asked him," said the father, "what are you doing here? School is not out yet."

"My son looked at me and stuttered, 'But Daddy, the man said, he said a missile was coming, that is what he said, "This missile is coming in five minutes." And so I wanted to get home before the missile.'"

"I just looked at him and said, 'The principal only meant to announce that dismissal was coming. Dismissal means that you can leave. That is all it means. There is no missile there.'"

"And then I brought him back to you. He shouldn't have left the school and crossed the street by himself. He won't do it again. I explained it to him."

I have to tell you that I wanted to take that boy's little *keppele* (that is "head" in Yiddish) and kiss his sweet face, but I figured he had had enough drama for the afternoon. See what I mean about language.

2. HUH?

In my day, the secretaries used to type up reports for the school personnel. Now everyone has their own computer, so they type for themselves. Once in a while, though, one of the staff will ask me to type something up, and what follows are some of the words I've encountered. Have you ever heard of them?

SPED, IEP, 504, SST, OT, PT, transitional specialist, life skills classroom, ELL, ESL, MTEL, DOE, SEI, PDPs, MELT Initiative, TBE, SES, ELP-BO, PIC, PBIS, FLEP, BAS, PE, DRA, MAPS, WIDA, on the spectrum, inclusion, time on task, DSE, PD, MEPA, MELA-O, BICS, TELL, extended evaluation, working memory, executive function, phonemic awareness, decoding, benchmarks, differentiated instruction, response to intervention, proficiency, rubric, portfolio. Oh, and accommodation, charter school, pilot school, magnet school. Do you understand those words?

Oh, yes, numeracy? That is different from mathematics or arithmetic, but how?

Prompts, cues, verbal/nonverbal audio protocol, scaffolding . . . seems that there is a "building" model.

Parents come in and ask me to explain. What am I supposed to say to them? They ask me because they are embarrassed to show the teacher or the psychologist that they don't know. "Mrs. Chapiro," that's what they call me, and they say, "Should I just sign this or what?" I tell them not to sign a thing until someone explains word for word what it means. Who knows what is going on with all this?

3. EMERGENCY NUMBERS PLEASE

There are a good number of things I did not learn at secretarial school, but in my early life, I grew up with old people from an old world, and so I learned to decipher an English language unknown to any university. This is important, so hear me out.

Once I worked in a big office in the big administration building downtown. Big, big, everyone there thinks they are big shots. One of the other secretaries would put on hold anyone with an accent, and then she would call one of the Spanish-speaking secretaries. It made no sense to me, and I would tell her, "Slow down, Carol, take a breath, just listen, tell the parent to speak slowly, that's all, you'll get it." But no, she would freeze, and then the parent who might be speaking Twi or Albanian would have to go through the whole rigmarole again. Ridiculous. All it would have taken would be a little training, though probably some people are like cats and can't be trained.

Not knowing English is a problem, but it's not a disability. You don't have to shout. Smile, and talk quietly and slowly, that's all. Parents are watching your face. Your face says it all. You could be talking sweetly, but if there is some way that your eyes are rolling because names seem strange, just can it. Oh, and something else, emergency numbers.

You are going to ask a new parent to fill out an emergency card. I have noticed that just saying the word *emergency* sends a chill into the office. Some families' entire existences have been an emergency, if you know what I mean. Camps, wars, run here, run there, move again, social and welfare workers, refugee and resettlement papers. You ask for two emergency phone numbers of people who don't know anyone with a phone. Now what?

And while we are at it, keep some candy in your drawer. While you are patiently trying to explain to a group of people what we need from them, there will be some babies or grandparents waiting. Feed them a little treat. It won't hurt, and maybe it will help. There are usually more people than usual in the office, as it has become clear to me that newcomers never travel alone. The world is too frightening.

4. ARE YOU HUNGRY?/JUST FILL OUT THESE FORMS

Students are sometimes told that there will be no special treat on Friday until everyone in the class brings in the lunch forms. I've had kids crying in front of my desk because they didn't bring in the paper. I'll tell you, my Grandma Ida's citizenship paper was less complicated than the lunch forms.

All you need to know is your income, net and gross. All you need to do is honestly report all sources of income. Make sure that you know how much you receive from SNAP, TANF, and FDPIR.

If there is someone who is homeless in your household, someone who has run away or is a migrant, make sure you keep them in mind. There is a spot for them on the RLF. Why would anyone want to tell their family's secrets to some unknown bureaucrat who gets to decide if your child eats lunch?

My granddaughter is a teacher, and she says that it's all about covering one's tuchus—layers and layers of words to show that the work was done. Fancy steps is what I call it.

In my day, things were plainer. Teachers knew who wasn't eating, and they made sure there was something for those students, even if it was just peanut butter and jelly. School was not so mysterious back then. Teachers said things like:

"Your son is not doing his work. If he doesn't start doing it, he won't pass to fourth grade."
"Debbie is doing the best she can, though it isn't really all that great. She is a sweet girl though."

Don't get me wrong: Things were not perfect back then by any means. There was a lot of yelling and sending kids to the office. There were many students who were forgotten, but there wasn't this layer of words on top of everything, if you know what I mean. These words are like extra-sweet-too-thick frosting. It kind of covers up all the imperfections, without really adding any . . . oomph.

FIFTY-ONE

letter to student

by Sarah Warren

this body is a transmitter

    twist of marrow
flesh
pink particles
      life is not
a pregnant mind or arms at an obtuse angle

it is an open palm, trick fingers that unravel
thick twine thread of truth

lies are in the absence
    between
    red bricks
    white walls
    black boards
      complex
cerebral cortex open wide

this is the torch to burn
these are the words to say
this is the braid to undo

    when I tell you
this clump in my throat is your honesty

FIFTY-TWO

Reflection Questions for Part Six: Advocacy and Solidarity

1. Writers in this section share stories about forging a sense of solidary in order to advocate for positive change or for the rights of individual students. What are some of the ways this happened?

2. Amy Vatne Bintliff writes in "Connecting with Carlos" about how she has been able to forge closer connections with many of her students through shared experiences of very different forms of pain. She shares that she decided no longer to hide from her students the evidence of her illness. How might these conditions help foster a sense of trust in her classroom?

About the Contributors

Hana Alhady, born in Slovenia, at age ten published a collection of her childhood poetry titled *My Blanket Covers Everything*. She also published several individual poems in various literary magazines and journals in Slovenia. The challenge of "interculturalism," which inspired her academic career, remains one of the major themes in her poetry.

Stacy Amaral taught bilingual classes in Worcester, Massachusetts, and in Managua, Nicaragua. She finished her school career as a counselor for foster homeless children and now works as an interpreter and writer. She has lived and worked in the same inner-city neighborhood for forty years.

Shannon Audley-Piotrowski is a former high school science teacher and currently works as an assistant professor of education and child study at Smith College. Her research interests focus on peer socialization and (dis)respect in primary and secondary classrooms.

Anne Beaton, a former high school English teacher, currently works as an instructional coach and leads district-level professional development. She has a PhD in curriculum and instruction.

Jehanne Beaton, after fourteen years of teaching secondary social studies in urban public school classrooms, works as a partnership liaison between an urban high school and university teacher education program, coaching and collaborating with teachers, novice and veteran, to better their instruction for diverse classrooms of teenagers. She is currently working on her doctorate in social studies education and teacher education.

Amy Vatne Bintliff is an educator and activist working in a reading classroom in Wisconsin. She is one of the 2014 Teaching Tolerance Award for Excellence in Teaching recipients. Her passions focus on restorative justice, building feelings of connectedness, and teaching reading and writing using an antibias framework.

Erin Bowers is a multidisciplinary artist specializing in mural and illustration work. She currently lives and works in Gainesville, Florida, with her friends and family.

Debra Busman is a fiction and creative nonfiction writer and professor at California State University, Monterey Bay, where she codirects the Creative Writing and Social Action Program. She coedited the book *Fire and Ink: An Anthology of Social Action Writing*. Her new novel, *like a woman*, was released in 2015.

Monique Cherry-McDaniel was a secondary English teacher for seven years and is currently an assistant professor and program coordinator for the Integrated Language Arts Program at Central State University, Wilberforce, Ohio. Her research and scholarship focuses primarily on teaching the canon and other literature in socially just and culturally responsive ways.

Rebekah Cordova is a teacher educator at the University of Florida. She has been in education as a teacher, researcher, activist, and advocate for eighteen years. She currently resides in San Mateo, Florida.

Geetha Durairajan works as a professor in the department of evaluation at the English and Foreign Languages University. She is interested in education in multilingual contexts and in teacher education.

Walter Enloe is Gordon B. Sanders Chair in Education at Hamline University in St. Paul. He first lived in Japan in 1961 at age twelve, moving to Hiroshima in 1963. He returned years later for eight years to be principal and teacher at Hiroshima International School.

Mayra Evangelista is a student leader and has been involved with Padres & Jovenes Unidos for more than ten years. Through this time, she has learned about structural racism and racial disparities and how to organize her community for educational justice. She has a dog named Gizmo and lives in Denver, Colorado.

María Gabriel has worked as a PK–12 Latina educator in public education since 1997 in Northern Colorado. She has devoted her career to increasing access and opportunity for culturally and linguistically diverse students through direct student support, family engagement, professional development, and community-based educational research. Her joy in life is laughing and having fun with her two elementary-age daughters.

Margot Fortunato Galt spent more than thirty years working as a writer in the schools throughout Minnesota and the Dakotas. Two of her five books of nonfiction, *The Story in History* (1992) and *Circuit Writer* (2006), were published by Teachers & Writers Collaborative in New York. She currently teaches writing and humanities at the college level. She holds a PhD in American studies from the University of Minnesota.

Sarah Gilbertson, age twenty-seven, was born and raised in Moorhead, Minnesota. Sarah has previously achieved a BA degree in art and is currently studying to become an art teacher. She stays busy working with children at a local homeless shelter, mentoring students at a local middle school, and working as an independent photographer.

Sarita Gonzales believes the intersection of art and activism is a critical place for community survival. She is involved in community work and youth organizing in Arizona and nationally through her consulting company TruthSarita, LLC. She is also codirector of Spoken Futures, Inc., a youth space to address inequity in communities through poetry.

Paul C. Gorski is an activist, author, and educator whose life revolves around social justice, environmental justice, and animal rights causes. He teaches in the Social Justice and Human Rights Program at George Mason University. He lives in Falls Church, Virginia, with two cats, Unity and Buster.

Elizabeth Harlan-Ferlo is a poet, teacher, and group facilitator building justice and compassion through creative arts. She designed and taught courses in religion, ethics, and social justice at Oregon Episcopal School in Portland, where she also served as a lay chaplain for nine years. Read more at www.elizabethharlanferlo.com.

Mary Elizabeth Hayes is a doctoral student in language and literacy education at the University of Georgia, with previous studies in linguistics and work experience in education management. Her research interests include negotiation of the self in crisis in emergent bilinguals and the experiences of non-Hispanic minority teachers of Spanish as a foreign language.

Toby Jenkins is a visiting assistant professor at the University of Hawaii, Manoa. Her work focuses on the utility of culture as a politic of social survival, a tool of social change, and a transformative space of nontraditional knowledge production. She has authored two books: *My Culture, My Color, My Self: Heritage, Resilience and Community in the Lives of Young Adults* and *Family, Community, & Higher Education*.

Alejandro Jimenez is a twenty-six-year-old spoken-word poet, educator, and avid runner from Colima, Mexico. Arriving in the United States as an undocumented immigrant in 1995 and working the Oregon pear and cherry farms for more than ten years, he now resides in Denver, where he's a happy high school librarian and poetry teacher.

Korina Jocson is on the faculty in the College of Education at the University of Massachusetts, Amherst. Her research and teaching interests include youth literacies; urban education; and issues of equity, access, and inclusion, particularly among historically marginalized youth. Jocson is the author of *Youth Poets: Empowering Literacies In and Out of Schools*.

LouAnn Johnson is a poet, playwright, dog rescuer, and author of the bestseller *Dangerous Minds* (originally titled *My Posse Don't Do Homework*). Her most recent books include *Teaching Outside the Box* and the young adult novel *Muchacho*. At present, LouAnne teaches high school full time in rural New Mexico.

Stephanie Jones is a professor at the University of Georgia and is interested in the design of spaces in neighborhoods and schools where young people and grown-ups are encouraged to be creative, curious, and critical together.

Cathi LaMarche has contributed to more than twenty-five anthologies. As an eighth-grade composition teacher, college essay coach, novelist, and essayist, she spends most of her time immersed in the written word. She resides in Missouri with her husband, two children, and three dogs.

Julie Landsman is a retired teacher, writer, and teacher trainer. Her book *A White Teacher Talks about Race* is in its third printing. She enjoys working in schools and teaching creative writing to all age groups. Her latest book is *Growing up White: A Veteran Teacher Reflects on Racism.* She believes student voices can drive educational change.

Richard Levine, a retired teacher and Working Families Party activist, is the author of *The Cadence of Mercy, A Tide of a Hundred Mountains, That Country's Soul, A Language Full of Wars and Songs*, and *Snapshots from a Battle.* Listen to Levine's "The Talkin' Frackin' Blues" on YouTube at http://www.youtube.com/watch?v=2QCrTfxOBRo.

Cherise Martinez-McBride teaches English at Chabot College in Hayward, California, and also coaches new English teachers as a lecturer in University of California, Berkeley's, Multicultural Urban Secondary English Program. When she's not teaching, she enjoys quilting, all things DIY, and spending time with her husband, Michael, and daughters, Sarai and Nylah.

Jeff McCullers is the director of grants and program development for the school district of Lee County, Florida. His professional work focuses on authentic instruction and assessment, teacher leadership, and the unintended consequences of education policy.

Lani T. Montreal is a Filipina writer, educator, and rabble-rouser in Chicago, where she lives and loves with her multicultural, multispecies family. She teaches English, literature, and film courses at Malcolm X College, where she is also the English department chair. Lani has also been published in numerous anthologies and magazines, both print and online.

Kyle "Guante" Tran Myhre is a hip-hop artist, two-time National Poetry Slam champion, activist, and educator based in Minneapolis, Minnesota. See http://www.guante.info for more, or connect on Twitter at @elguante.

Kindel Nash is an assistant professor of urban teacher education and language and literacy at the University of Missouri, Kansas City. Her research interests include critical race theory and culturally relevant childhood literacy. She is thrilled to fulfill her lifelong goal of becoming a published poet!

Katrina Ohstrom, a photographer, has focused for the past several years on visually documenting the impact of austerity measures and free-market education reform. Using the backdrop of long-vacant public school buildings, newly shuttered classrooms, and school nurse's offices, Ohstrom challenges her audience to draw their own conclusions about the state of childhood, equality, and education in America today.

Kelly Jean Olivas has taught high school English in southern California "forever," where she lives with one husband, two daughters, three dogs, several lizards, and way too many ants at certain times of the year.

Mari Ann Roberts is an associate professor of multicultural education at Clayton State University in Morrow, Georgia. Her research interests include teacher care, critical race theory, and standardized testing abuse. In her spare time, she grades student papers, writes unruly poetry, and talks to her dog.

Janice Sapigao is a Pinay poet and writer from San Jose, California. She earned her MFA in critical studies/writing at CalArts. She cofounded an open mic in Los Angeles called Sunday Jump. She works at Skyline College and San Jose City College in the San Francisco Bay area. Visit her website: janicewrites.com.

Mary Harwell Sayler has placed three poetry books and two dozen books for all age groups with Christian and educational publishers. In addition, she's written three e-books to help other poets and writers, and she provides a variety of writing resources on her blogs and website.

Yvette A. Schnoeker-Shorb has worked as a GED-preparation facilitator, a college-level special-needs tutor, an adjunct undergraduate mentor, and a contracted graduate-thesis reader. She is cofounder and senior editor for Native West Press, a 501(c)(3) nonprofit natural history press. A past Pushcart Prize nominee, her poetry has appeared in numerous publications.

Julia Stein's seventh book of poetry, *What Were They Like?* was published March 2013. In her fourth book, *Walker Woman*, she wrote a long series of poems about teaching at Southwest College in south-central Los Angeles. She is adjunct professor at Santa Monica College, a community college.

Alison Stone wrote *Dangerous Enough, Borrowed Logic, From the Fool to the World*, and *They Sing at Midnight*, which won the 2003 Many Mountains Moving Award. She was awarded *Poetry*'s Frederick Bock Prize and *New York Quarterly*'s Madeline Sadin Award. She created the Stone Tarot and is a psychotherapist.

Cinthia Suasti has been a student leader with Padres and Jovenes Unidos since her junior year of high school. She recently graduated from Abraham Lincoln High School and is excited to keep working with the organization and going to community college in the near future.

V. Thandi Sulé is an assistant professor of higher education and the coordinator of the Master's in Higher Education Leadership Program at Oakland University. As a critical race scholar, her work focuses on educational equity issues, including access, retention, sense of belonging, and intercultural competencies. Poetry and prose are components of her scholarship.

Paul Thomas, associate professor of education (Furman University), taught high school English in South Carolina before moving to teacher education. He is currently a column editor for *English Journal* (National Council of Teachers of English) and coeditor of *Social Context Reform* (Routledge). Follow his work at http://radicalscholarship.wordpress.com and @plthomasEdD.

Thomas Turman is married with two daughters and a native Californian. He's written, practiced architecture, and taught in Berkeley for the last forty-five years. His work can be seen at http://www.thomasleeturman.com.

Sarah Warren is a writer, musician, and teacher. She has taught literature and writing classes (and music lessons) for eleven years at the collegiate and secondary levels. Sarah is currently working toward a PhD in English at the University of North Texas in Denton, Texas, and though she has lived in Texas since 2006, she will always identify as a native Oklahoman. Sarah teaches English composition at University of North Texas and also at Richland College in Dallas, Texas. She lives in Dallas with her dog and two cats.

James F. Woglom is an artist/educator who teaches at Humboldt State University. His research addresses arts-based research methodologies and furthering ideations of the arts as a means of affecting and promoting social change.

Andrena Zawinski, features editor at http://www.PoetryMagazine.com, is author of *Traveling in Reflected Light*, a Kenneth Patchen Prize in poetry. Her most recent collection, *Something About*, is a PEN Oakland Josephine Miles Award recipient. She hails from Pittsburgh, Pennsylvania, but has made her home in the San Francisco Bay area.

www.ingramcontent.com/pod-product-compliance
Lightning Source LLC
Chambersburg PA
CBHW021815270326
41932CB00007B/200